Date Due

Demco 293-5

Development of
Marketing Theory

GEORGE SCHWARTZ, Ph.D.

College of Business Administration
The University of Rochester, New York

SOUTH-WESTERN PUBLISHING CO.

Cincinnati 27   Chicago 44   New Rochelle, N. Y.   Dallas 2
                              Burlingame, Calif.

G61

41308

Copyright ©, 1963

by

South-Western Publishing Company
Cincinnati 27, Ohio

Library of Congress Catalog Card Number 63-13358

K163
Printed in the United States of America

PREFACE

•

This book is a study in marketing theory. It seeks to determine the extent to which empirically valid marketing theory has thus far been developed and to make suggestions for the future development of marketing theory.

The author is indebted to Dr. Reavis Cox, Food Fair Foundation Professor of Marketing at the Wharton School of Finance and Commerce, who stimulated the author's interest in marketing theory and who offered many helpful suggestions which substantially facilitated the completion of this study. Appreciation is also expressed to Dr. Francis E. Brown of the Wharton School's Statistics Department who gave unselfishly of his time to aid the author with his statistical problems, as did Dr. Edwin B. Cox of Boston University.

George Schwartz

EDITOR'S SERIES

We are proud to present in the Editor's Series books that we feel should be available to the profession.

Books in this series are selected and published because of their scholarly nature, their contribution to advanced thinking and research, or their general professional contribution to the improvement of business and economic education. Appropriate manuscripts will be considered on their merit.

Books of the Editor's Series are those that every professionally minded person will want to possess. They should be in every library. Most of them will be useful as supplemental readings for students.

CONTENTS

TABLES

ILLUSTRATIONS

Chapter 1

TOWARD THE DEVELOPMENT OF MARKETING THEORIES*

Students of marketing generally date the genesis of the serious study of marketing at approximately 1900. Since that date many facts and much descriptive material relating to the activities and institutions of marketing have been published. It is generally thought that this aspect of the study of marketing has been covered quite thoroughly.[1]

The relative adequacy of the factual fund of marketing knowledge has not, however, proved sufficient to satisfy a number of marketing students and practitioners who are of the opinion that development of marketing theory is both possible and useful. For a number of these individuals the plethora of facts "seem to add up to very little."[2] Other students of marketing, while similarly of the opinion that development of marketing theory is desirable, have concluded that this goal cannot be attained.[3]

Growing Interest in Marketing Theory

Interest in the development of marketing theory and discussion of the feasibility of such an objective is of relatively recent origin. A historical sampling of marketing literature indicates that prior to 1941 only a few marketing students and practitioners devoted any considerable attention to theory. For the most part "scientific marketing literature" related to the application to marketing of methods and

---

*Most of this chapter appeared as an article in the *University of Washington Business Review*, Vol. XXI (April–June, 1962), pp. 57–63.

[1]Another view holds that while marketing students have collected many facts, these are not always the right facts or the facts which can lead to analysis. The opinion stated above in the text is restricted to the available fund of factual information on marketing in the United States. The investigation of domestic marketing abroad by students in the United States has not been carried far, and the available information on this aspect of marketing is meager.

[2]See, for example, Wroe Alderson and Reavis Cox, "Towards a Theory of Marketing," *Journal of Marketing*, national quarterly publication of the American Marketing Association, Vol. XIII (October, 1948), p. 138.

[3]K. D. Hutchinson, "Marketing as a Science: An Appraisal," *Journal of Marketing*, national quarterly publication of the American Marketing Association, Vol. XVI (January, 1952), pp. 289–290.

analytical tools used successfully by F. W. Taylor in increasing the efficiency of production.[4]

Much of this literature concentrated on the marketing problems of an individual company and emphasized that: (1) the day of the rule of thumb in selling was over and (2) scientific and exact knowledge must replace it. One author, however, wrote that scientific marketing involved teaching children and their parents how to compute weights and prices instead of taking the word of the butcher on these "important points." This author suggested that a number of retired butchers and bakers were available as lecturers for this purpose.[5]

That serious interest in marketing theory was apparently lacking prior to the last two decades is indicated in a study by Robert Bartels. After an intensive search of the marketing literature, Bartels concluded that "relatively few principles of marketing have been presented."[6]

Walter Dill Scott, an early student of marketing theory, displayed an understanding of theory and science which would be acceptable to many a present-day marketing theoretician. In a book on the theory and practice of advertising published in 1908, Scott wrote about the experimental method, probability, and prediction in connection with the use of psychology and media space in advertising. He wrote, for example:

> Other things being equal, the probabilities that any particular thing will catch our attention are in proportion to the absence of competing attractions. This seems to indicate that, other things being equal, the full-page advertisement is the "sure-to-be-seen" advertisement, and that the size of an advertisement determines the number of chances it has of being seen.[7]

The work of William J. Reilly aimed at formulating a principle for the establishment of retail market areas for shopping goods is, of course, a widely recognized early contribution to marketing science.[8] In addition, the formation during the 1930's of the American Marketing

---

[4]Examples of this literature are: Amasa Walker, "Scientific Management Applied to Commercial Enterprise," *Journal of Political Economy* (May, 1913), pp. 388–399; Percival White, *Scientific Marketing Management* (New York: Harper & Brothers, 1927); Henry P. Kendall, "Applying the Laws of Production to Distribution," *Printer's Ink* (May 15, 1930).

[5]"Scientific Marketing—A New Branch of Education," *Outlook* (September 23, 1914).

[6]Robert Bartels, "Marketing Literature—Development and Appraisal" (Ph.D. dissertation, Ohio State University, 1941), pp. 385–86.

[7]Walter D. Scott, *The Theory and Practice of Advertising* (Boston: Small, Maynard & Co., 1908), pp. 9–10.

[8]William J. Reilly, *The Law of Retail Gravitation* (1st ed.; Austin: University of Texas Press, 1931).

Society and the National Association of Marketing Teachers, which later merged to form the American Marketing Association, stimulated the development of marketing theory. Each of these organizations had as one of its major objectives the promotion of the scientific study of marketing.[9]   Since its formation in 1936, the American Marketing Association has encouraged and facilitated the development of marketing science by sponsoring conferences and aiding in the publication of studies focussing on marketing theory.

Bartels' study, completed in 1941, represents a relatively important contribution to the literature of marketing theory. Not only did Bartels make an intensive search of the literature for marketing principles, but he also studied the conceptual, methodological, and other problems involved in developing marketing theory and science.[10]

Bartels' contribution was followed by the publication in 1948 of a significant article by Wroe Alderson and Reavis Cox.[11] The importance of this article lay in the fact that it apparently stimulated discussion and research in the area of marketing theory.

Following publication of the Alderson and Cox article, the American Marketing Association sponsored the preparation of a symposium on theory in marketing which was published in 1950.[12] Other symposiums were published shortly thereafter such as those edited by Hugh G. Wales, Schuyler F. Otteson, and Stewart H. Rewoldt.[13] In addition to these edited works, several books have been published representing individual contributions to marketing theory by Henry H. Bakken, Edward A. Duddy and David A. Revzan, Geoffrey S. Shephard, Ralph F. Breyer, and Wroe Alderson.[14]

---

[9]See, for example, the statement by L. D. H. Weld, President, American Marketing Society, published in the *American Marketing Journal* (January, 1934), p. 5.

[10]Bartels, *loc. cit.* See also, Robert Bartels, "Marketing Principles," *Journal of Marketing*, national quarterly publication of the American Marketing Association, Vol. IX (October, 1944). Bartels' review of marketing literature was brought up-to-date in his book, *Development of Marketing Thought* (Homewood, Illinois: Richard D. Irwin, Inc., 1962).

[11]Alderson and Cox, *loc. cit.*

[12]Reavis Cox and Wroe Alderson (eds.) *Theory in Marketing* (Homewood, Illinois: Richard D. Irwin, Inc., 1950).

[13]H. G. Wales (ed.), *Changing Perspectives in Marketing* (Urbana: University of Illinois Press, 1951). S. F. Otteson (ed.) *Marketing: Current Problems and Theories* (Bloomington: Indiana University Press, 1952). S. H. Rewoldt (ed.), *Frontiers in Marketing Thought* (Bloomington: Indiana University Press, 1954).

[14]H. H. Bakken, *Theory of Markets and Marketing* (Madison, Wisconsin: Mimir Publishers, Inc., 1953). E. A. Duddy and D. A. Revzan, *Marketing: An Institutional Approach* (New York: McGraw-Hill Book Company, 1953). G. S. Shepherd, *Marketing Farm Products—Economic Analysis* (Ames: Iowa State College Press, 1955). R. F. Breyer, *Quantitative Systemic Analysis and Control: Study No. 1 Channel and Channel Group Costing* (Philadelphia: Published by the author, photo-offset, 1949). W. Alderson, *Marketing Behavior and Executive Action* (Homewood, Illinois: Richard D. Irwin, Inc., 1957).

The growing interest in theory among marketing students has also been evidenced by articles which appeared from time to time in various journals, monographs, and other publications.[15] In addition to these, Weldon J. Taylor and William C. McInnes have recently written Ph.D. theses in the area of marketing theory,[16] and Ralph B. Thompson has collected a list of sources which, in his opinion, represents a "bibliography of marketing theory."[17] It should also be noted that in June 1962 the Marketing Science Institute was formed with the financial support of 29 corporations. In an early statement of its goals, the Institute announced that it would conduct research and education activities designed (1) to contribute to the emergence of a more definitive science of marketing and (2) to stimulate increased application of scientific techniques to the understanding and solving of marketing problems.

Is Development of Marketing Theory Practicable?

A fundamental question which has received serious consideration in the growing literature of marketing theory has been whether development of such theory is practicable. A number of marketing students do not concern themselves with this question but appear to presuppose that attainment of this objective is feasible. Others, however, have focused on this question and have taken either affirmative or negative positions.

Among those on the negative side of this question, several have expressed sharply unequivocal opinions. Kenneth D. Hutchinson, for example, has written that it is the drollest travesty to relate the scientist's search for knowledge to the market research man's seeking after customers.[18] Similarly, John E. Jeuck has asserted that it is a delusion to think that marketing is or can be a science.[19]

Both Hutchinson and Jeuck believe that marketing is an art.

---

[15]Among those making such contributions are the following: Paul D. Converse, Roland S. Vaile, E. T. Grether, John E. Jeuck, Lawrence C. Lockley, Stanley C. Hollander, Melvin Anshen, P. J. Verdoorn, William J. Baumol, and George Fisk.

[16]W. J. Taylor, "A Critical Analysis of a Standard for Creating Scientific Objectives in the Study of Marketing and the Application of Such Standard to Contemporary Marketing Literature" (Ph.D. dissertation, New York University, 1955). William C. McInnes, "A General Theory of Marketing" (Ph.D. dissertation, New York University, 1954).

[17]R. B. Thompson, *Marketing Theory: a selected and annotated bibliography* (Austin: University of Texas Press, 1958).

[18]K. D. Hutchinson, "Marketing as a Science: An Appraisal," *Journal of Marketing*, national quarterly publication of the American Marketing Association, Vol. XVI (January, 1952), p. 290.

[19]John E. Jeuck, "Marketing Research—Milestone or Millstone?," *Journal of Marketing*, national quarterly publication of the American Marketing Association, Vol. XIII (April, 1953), p. 382.

Hutchinson bases his position on the assertion that the solution of each problem in marketing requires a different and distinct combination of techniques,[20] while Jeuck writes that marketing success depends more upon the imaginative and aggressive personality than upon the results of research.[21] Roland S. Vaile also holds that marketing is an art, basing his opinion on the importance which he attaches to the "unpredictable" nature of innovation and extravaganza in marketing.[22] Despite these views, both Hutchinson and Vaile are of the opinion that theories developed in the various social sciences such as economics, psychology, and sociology can be useful in the practice of marketing.

Other students who doubt that marketing theory can be developed emphasize that human behavior extends over a wide range and is not static. For these reasons, they state, laws cannot be formulated which will accurately predict human behavior.[23]

McGarry, though he believes that development of marketing theory is possible, doubts that such theory will enable marketing analysts or practitioners to predict with the accuracy of physics or chemistry. The reason for this, he states, is that most of the important factors involved in marketing are difficult to define and impossible to measure.[24] Stanley Hollander also believes that development of marketing theory is practicable but is of the opinion that the social aspects of marketing are more amenable to scientific study than is the case with its acquisitive aspects. This is so, he writes, because (1) subjectivity declines as truth rather than profits become the goal and (2) in the study of the social aspects of marketing, the pressure of deadlines lessens and sufficient leisure may be obtained to maintain perspective.[25]

Among those students of marketing who believe that marketing

---

[20]Hutchinson, *loc. cit.*

[21]Jeuck, *op. cit.*. p. 384.

[22]R. S. Vaile, "Towards a Theory of Marketing—A Comment," *Journal of Marketing* (April, 1949), p. 522. See also R. S. Vaile, "Science Applied to Advertising," *Journal of Marketing*, national quarterly publication of the American Marketing Association, Vol. XIII (July, 1955), p. 48.

[23]Examples of this position can be seen in Amasa Walker's "Scientific Management Applied to Commercial Enterprise," *Journal of Political Economy* (May, 1913), p. 392. See also, L. J. Raymond, "Direct Advertising Also Favors Scientific Marketing," *Journal of Marketing* (January, 1937), p. 267.

[24]Edmund D. McGarry, "Dean Lockley's Advertising Principles," *Journal o Marketing*, national quarterly publication of the American Marketing Association' Vol. XIX (April, 1955), p. 353. Robert S. Stainton also points to the impossibility of measuring all of the important variables in marketing as a barrier to the development of marketing science. See R. S. Stainton, "Science in Marketing," *Journal of Marketing*, national quarterly publication of the American Marketing Association, Vol. XVII (July, 1952), p. 65.

[25]S. C. Hollander, "The Limitations of Science in the Study and Practice of Marketing," in S. H. Rewoldt (ed.)., *Frontiers in Marketing Thought* (Bloomington: Indiana University Press, 1954), p. 184.

theory can be developed, Bartels is one of the most articulate. In Bartels' opinion marketing may be regarded either as science or art. However, to regard marketing as art, Bartels writes, is to emphasize the doing rather than the knowing. According to him the art of marketing is the technical, professional, applicative aspect of the subject. By contrast, marketing as science consists of the body of knowledge of distribution with its theories, laws, principles, and concepts. It is Bartels' view that such a science can be developed if marketing students will utilize appropriate methods of study.[26]

Bartels also disputes the assertion that theory in marketing is not practicable because human behavior cannot be predicted. While he acknowledges that this is true to some extent in individual cases, he asserts that the stability of the behavior of groups and the tendency of individuals to conform to the group pattern constitute a uniformity sufficient for making valid and reliable predictions.[27]

The belief that theory in marketing is likely to come from students of the social sciences is rejected by William J. Baumol. Baumol's position is that theories from the social sciences should be used as "bricks for the construction of marketing theory rather than constituting its sum and substance."[28] Baumol emphasizes that the appropriate choice of theory is a matter of the problem in which the investigator is interested, and he asserts that since marketing has its special problems, students of the field may find it useful to develop their own body of theory.[29]

Theodore H. Brown refuses to accept the argument that the large number of marketing variables and the difficulty of their measurement raises doubts as to whether theory in marketing can be developed. He holds that if this argument were accepted research advances in most fields of knowledge would stop "almost immediately."[30] To support his view that marketing science can be developed, an early student of marketing asserts his belief in natural law. W. C. Holman, writing in 1913, maintains that millions of daily phenomena are all under the rule of fixed laws. It is not conceivable to him "that the creator who

[26]Robert Bartels, "Can Marketing Be a Science," *Journal of Marketing*, national quarterly publication of the American Marketing Association, Vol. XV (January 1951), pp. 322–23.
[27]*Ibid.*, p. 320.
[28]W. J. Baumol, "On the Role of Marketing Theory," *Journal of Marketing*, national quarterly publication of the American Marketing Association, Vol. XXI (April, 1957), p. 417.
[29]*Ibid.*
[30]T. H. Brown, "Science, Statistics, and Business," *Harvard Business Review* (Autumn, 1937), p. 282.

made the universe — ruled in every other of its billions of facts and phases by laws and principles should leave one tiny area of chaos, and that, the advertising and selling of goods."[31]

Objectives of the Study

In undertaking this study, the writer presupposes that the development of marketing theory is possible. Although he does not know that the discovery of marketing theory is possible, he is willing to make this presupposition because: (1) he is not sure that it can be proven that the discovery of marketing theory is impossible and (2) he believes that the discovery of such theory is likely to be useful to marketing students, to marketing practitioners, and to government officials concerned with marketing.

This study analyzes a number of approaches to the development of marketing theory in order to answer the question: What progress has been achieved in the development of marketing theory through use of certain major theoretical approaches?

The theoretical approaches evaluated in this study are examined through the relevant publications of Wroe Alderson, Ralph Breyer, Paul D. Converse, Reavis Cox, Charles S. Goodman, Ewald T. Grether, Edmund D. McGarry, Oskar Morgenstern, William J. Reilly, John Q. Stewart, John von Neumann, and William Warntz. The approaches of these theorists, some of whom are not known as students of marketing, have been selected for study because each constitutes a recognized and unique approach to the development of marketing theory.

Reilly's approach is empirical, aimed at formulating a regression equation which gives acceptably accurate predictions. Converse has used a similar approach.

Stewart is an astophysicist who is now studying social phenomena. He and William Warntz are in the forefront of a group which is attempting to build a science called social physics. Social physics was selected for study in this book because some of its concepts, variables, and methodology appear to have utility in the development of marketing theory.

The late John von Neumann was known as one of the foremost mathematicians in the United States. He initiated development of the theory of games of strategy which he later, in association with an economist Oskar Morgenstern, applied to economic problems. The theory of

---

[31]W. C. Holman, "Guess-Work in Advertising," *System* (August, 1913), p. 176.

games is studied in this book because it exemplifies the use of mathematical models in the development of marketing theory.

Grether is included because he is noted for the use of the deductive approach of economic theory as a springboard for the development of marketing theory. The functional approach to the development of marketing theory is evaluated in this book through analysis of the work of McGarry. This approach spotlights the activities performed in marketing.

Alderson calls his approach the functionalist approach. His approach seeks to develop marketing theory by identifying a system of action and then determining how and why it works as it does.

Breyer's approach has been named the systemic approach. It studies various aspects of marketing with respect to and from the point of view of marketing channels, which he regards as systems. A study by Cox and Goodman is included in this study because it constitutes an experiment in research methodology.

Each of these approaches is evaluated in the following chapters to determine the extent to which each has enabled the theorist using it to develop empirically valid marketing theory. After these analyses have been completed, the writer presents his views on the second question posed by this study: How can marketing theory best be developed in the future?

In essence, this study seeks to answer the question: Where are we with respect to the development of marketing theory, and where do we go from here?

It should be noted that the formulation of a marketing theory is not an objective of this study.

Chapter 2

LAWS OF RETAIL GRAVITATION*

William J. Reilly and Paul D. Converse are well known for their work on the problem of retail trade area determination. The efforts of both have focused on developing mathematical formulas which would enable marketing practitioners to delineate trade areas and analyze the movement of retail trade without having to perform expensive field work.[1]

Approach to Marketing Theory

While any comprehensive discussion of marketing theory is not likely to omit the names of Reilly and Converse, neither has written much explicitly detailing his concepts of such matters as science, law, or theory. In what little he has written on these questions, Reilly distinguishes between theory and law, and Converse has published scattered comments on theory and science.

Reilly views theory as an attempt to explain something on the basis of what is thought might be true. It is merely an explanation, he states, which can be disputed by anyone until such time as its truth is demonstrated by scientific measurement.[2] A law, however, is based on the measurement of actual conditions which no one can dispute.[3] Such measurement summarizes existing conditions in a form which enables

---

*Most of this chapter appeared as an article in the *University of Washington Business Review*, Vol. XXII (October, 1962), pp. 53–70.

[1]In addition to his work in this area, Converse's attempts to estimate the global cost of marketing for 1929, 1939, and 1948 also represent significant contributions to marketing science. See P. D. Converse and H. W. Huegy, *Elements of Marketing* (2nd ed.; New York: Prentice-Hall, Inc., 1942), p. 817; P. D. Converse, "The Total Cost of Marketing," *Journal of Marketing* (April, 1946), p. 389; and P. D. Converse, H. W. Huegy, and R. V. Mitchell, *Elements of Marketing* (6th ed.; New York: Prentice-Hall, Inc., 1958), p. 742.

[2]Reilly's concept of theory is, of course, similar to the concept of hypothesis held by other students of science.

[3]W. J. Reilly, *The Law of Retail Gravitation* (1st ed.; New York: William J. Reilly Company, 1931), p. 32. This book was reprinted, virtually unchanged, in 1953.

prediction. A law need not predict accurately in all situations. Exceptions to a law are considered abnormal.[4]

Converse views theory as illustrated by economic theory with skepticism. In his view many human actions are not logical, and he speculates that perhaps man's emotions are more important than his logic. For Converse, "economic theories gave us a starting point — or a series of hypotheses."[5] If such hypotheses did not apply, he attempted to find out how the theories had to be modified, or what new ones had to be formulated.[6]

Converse's use of Reilly's law in his studies of the movement of retail trade demonstrates that his concept of law is similar to Reilly's. In Converse's view exceptions do not overthrow a law, and the accuracy of a law is measured by computing a coefficient of correlation relating the extent of co-variation between the law's predictions and fact determined by consumer surveys.[7] He does not state the extent to which the value of such a coefficient would have to depart from 1 in order to lead him to conclude that a statement was not a law.

Converse views science as an organized body of knowledge dealing with a body of facts or truths systematically arranged. Although he does not explain the basis for his view, he writes that marketing meets the specifications of this concept and "so can rightfully be called a science."[8]

The Laws of Retail Gravitation

The several laws of retail gravitation which now appear in marketing literature have their genesis in the analysis of retail trade undertaken in 1927 by Reilly. His studies were conducted over a period of more than three years and had as their objective the discovery of some method for measuring the retail trade influence of a city.[9] Converse's

---

[4]*Ibid.*, pp. 33–34.

[5]Paul D. Converse, "Development of Marketing Theory: Fifty Years of Progress," published in Hugh G. Wales (ed.), *Changing Perspectives in Marketing* (Urbana: University of Illinois Press, 1951), p. 2.

[6]*Ibid.*

[7]Paul D. Converse, *A Study of Retail Trade Areas in East Central Illinois*, (Urbana: University of Illinois Press, 1943), pp. 44–48.

[8]Converse, "Development of Marketing Theory: Fifty Years of Progress," published in Wales (ed.), *op. cit.*, p. 31. Some students of science maintain that a body of knowledge does not constitute a science until it has: (1) systematically organized the facts pertaining to the specific field of study and (2) developed useful concepts, theories, principles, and laws.

[9]Reilly, *op. cit.*, p. 56. Reilly defines "retail trade influence of a city" as the amount of retail trade a city draws from its surrounding area.

work has centered on refining the results of Reilly's studies and developing new measures of the movement of retail trade among cities.

The studies conducted by Reilly and Converse have led to the development of six formulas which are termed laws of retail gravitation. The original law developed by Reilly states:

> Two cities attract retail trade[10] from any intermediate city or town in the vicinity of the breaking point[11] approximately in direct proportion to the population of the two cities and in inverse proportion to the square of the distances from these two cities to the intermediate town.[12]

This statement can be expressed mathematically as follows:

$$\frac{B_a}{B_b} = \left(\frac{P_a}{P_b}\right)\left(\frac{D_b}{D_a}\right)^2 \dots\dots\dots\dots\dots\dots\dots\dots\dots\dots\dots (1)$$

1. B_a is the proportion of retail trade from the intermediate town attracted by city A.
2. B_b is the proportion attracted by city B.
3. P_a is the population of city A.
4. P_b is the population of city B.
5. D_a is the distance from the intermediate town to city A.
6. D_b is the distance from the intermediate town to city B.

In presenting this law, Reilly wrote that the law, like many other discoveries, may at first be discarded as incredible. "In spite of the fact that the law is merely a summarized statement of existing conditions," he writes, "it will probably be criticized as 'theoretical' by some who loosely use that word and who will not even bother to read the description of how the law was discovered."[13]

---

[10]By retail trade, Reilly apparently means purchases of shopping goods, specialty goods, and convenience goods. See *ibid.*, pp. 64–69. Converse uses the term retail trade to refer to purchases of shopping goods, principally fashion goods. According to Converse, people attach great importance to the purchasing of shopping goods. They are usually goods of large unit value, goods which are important in the family budget. Many of them are purchased at infrequent intervals, and the purchases are usually planned long in advance. In the purchase of fashion goods, the typical consumer wants something distinctive, something to suit a specific need or individual taste. In the search for fashion newness, consumers may visit several stores and are willing to travel considerable distances to reach stores with stocks large enough to give them assortments from which to choose, according to Converse. Fashion goods consist of apparel, furniture, jewelry, luggage, and gift goods. Coats, hats, dresses, and shoes for women, and rugs, and draperies for the home head the list. See Paul D. Converse, *Retail Trade Areas in Illinois* (Urbana: University of Illinois Press, 1946).

[11]Reilly defines a breaking point as a point up to which one city exercises the dominating retail trade influence, and beyond which the other city dominates.

[12]Reilly, *op. cit.*, p.9.

[13]*Ibid.*, p. 6.

The second formula used to measure the movement of shopping goods trade was developed by Converse and his associates. It is known as the "breaking point" formula and is written as follows:

$$D_b = \frac{D_a + D_b}{1 + \sqrt{\dfrac{P_a}{P_b}}} \quad \dots\dots\dots\dots\dots\dots \quad (2)$$

In this formula the "breaking point" between any two cities is the intermediate community which divides its shopping goods trade equally between the two cities.

Formula (2) was derived from formula (1). While Converse does not demonstrate how this was done, the mathematical procedure involved can be shown as follows:

1. $\dfrac{B_a}{B_b} = \left(\dfrac{P_a}{P_b}\right)\left(\dfrac{D_b}{D_a}\right)^2$

   at a breaking point $\dfrac{B_a}{B_b} = 1$

$\therefore$ 2. $1 = \left(\dfrac{P_a}{P_b}\right)\left(\dfrac{D_b}{D_a}\right)^2$

3. D the distance between A and B equals $D_a + D_b$

4. $D_a = D - D_b$

5. $1 = \left(\dfrac{P_a}{P_b}\right)\left(\dfrac{D_b}{D - D_b}\right)^2$

6. $\dfrac{P_b}{P_a} = \left(\dfrac{D_b}{D - D_b}\right)^2$

7. $\dfrac{D_b}{D - D_b} = \sqrt{\dfrac{P_b}{P_a}}$

8. $D_b = D - D_b\sqrt{\dfrac{P_b}{P_a}}$

9. $D_b = D\sqrt{\dfrac{P_b}{P_a}} - D_b\sqrt{\dfrac{P_b}{P_a}}$

10. $D\sqrt{\dfrac{P_b}{P_a}} = D_b + D_b\sqrt{\dfrac{P_b}{P_a}}$

11. $D\sqrt{\dfrac{P_b}{P_a}} = D_b\left(1 + \sqrt{\dfrac{P_b}{P_a}}\right)$

12. $D_b = \dfrac{D\sqrt{\dfrac{P_b}{P_a}}}{1 + \sqrt{\dfrac{P_b}{P_a}}}$

Multiplying the right side of equation 12 by $\sqrt{\dfrac{P_a}{P_b}}$ yields equation

13. $D_b = \dfrac{D}{1 + \sqrt{\dfrac{P_a}{P_b}}}$ which is the same as formula (2), i.e.,

14. Breaking point, miles from B =

$$\dfrac{\text{Miles between } A \text{ and } B}{1 + \sqrt{\dfrac{\text{Population of } A}{\text{Population of } B}}}$$

According to Converse, formula (2) can be used to determine the boundaries of a town's normal trading area without performing any field work.[14]   Distances are measured by improved automobile highways. In bounding the trade area of a city, the population is considered in relation to the population of competing towns and the distances separating them. Thus, if city A has a population of 120,000 and is 75 miles from city B which has a population of 30,000, the breaking point between their trading areas will be approximately 25 miles from city B. After a city's trading area is delimited, formula (1) then can be used to determine how the retail trade should be divided between two trading centers.[15]

---

[14]This applies to trading relations between towns or cities where the difference in population is relatively small. It does not apply, for example, to trading relations between a metropolis and its small suburbs.

[15]When Converse states that formula (1) can be used to determine how retail trade should be divided between two trading centers, he means that a prediction resulting from use of this formula represents a division of trade which would exist if the forces determining this division were average. While he does not so state, it appears that this latter statement stems from the method used by Reilly in developing formula (1). This method is described below starting on page 16. The same considerations lead him to use the term normal in describing the trading area which is determined by use of formula (2).

If the actual movement of retail trade in a specific situation as determined by a consumer survey differs from that predicted by formulas (1) and (2), Converse would conclude that the shopping goods merchants in the relevant trading centers were obtaining more or less of the trade from the surrounding area than average. For example, if city *A* received 45 per cent of the shopping goods trade from a town located on the periphery of its trading area as determined by formula (2), Converse would conclude that the shopping goods merchants in city *A* needed to take promotional action in order to raise this figure to at least 50 per cent.

Another law of retail gravitation developed by Converse states:

> A trading center and a town in or near its trade area divide the trade of the town approximately in direct proportion to the populations of the two towns and inversely as the squares of the distance factors, using 4 as the distance factor of the home town.[16]

This statement can be expressed mathematically as follows:

$$\frac{B_a}{B_b} = \left(\frac{P_a}{H_b}\right)\left(\frac{4}{d}\right)^2 \dots\dots\dots\dots\dots\dots \quad (3)$$

1. B_a is the proportion of trade going to the outside town.[17]
2. B_b is the proportion of trade retained by the home town.
3. P_a is the population of the outside town.
4. H_b is the population of the home town.
5. d is the distance to the outside town.
6. 4 is the inertia factor.[18]

According to Converse, formula (3) can be used as follows: Suppose that the relative division of fashion goods purchases made by residents of a town in the town and in a nearby trading center is determined by a consumer survey, i.e., B_a and B_b are known. Since P_a, H_b, and d are known, formula (3) can be solved for the value of the inertia-distance factor.[19] If the computed inertia-distance factor exceeded 4, Converse

---

[16]Paul D. Converse, "New Laws of Retail Gravitation," *Journal of Marketing*, national quarterly publication of the American Marketing Association, Vol. XIV (October, 1949), p. 382.

[17]It would appear that Converse means fashion goods trade since the formula is based on data reflecting the movement of fashion goods purchases.

[18]The inertia-distance factor, according to Converse, reflects the inertia that must be overcome to visit a store which is even one block away. Converse conjectures that the purchases, not made in the nearby large city because of this inertia factor, are made either in the home town or in shopping centers in the suburbs of the large city.

[19]P_a and H_b can be obtained from census data, if these are not out of date, or estimated on the basis of relevant demographic data. The value of d can be obtained from a highway map. In this instance d would equal the distance between the home town and the outside town by way of the best road connecting the two.

would conclude that the proportion of fashion goods trade retained by the merchants of the home town was below average and that, perhaps, a program aimed at inducing residents to make more of their fashion goods purchases in the home town was in order.

If a small town loses a considerable amount of trade to two or more larger towns, the proportion lost to these towns is, according to Converse, determined by using multiples of 4 to obtain a total inertia factor. If "Doeville" loses trade to two large towns, Converse would use 8 as the inertia factor. If "Doeville" loses trade to three, he would use 12; and if it loses trade to four towns, he would use 16. Converse states that he has experimented with this method, and he has concluded that it appears to work satisfactorily.

Two additional laws of retail gravitation developed by Converse are basically similar to formulas (1) and (2). They represent modifications of these formulas in order to increase predictive accuracy in situations where a trading center is more than 20 times the size of a relevant intermediate town. These formulas are:

$$\frac{B_a}{B_b} = \left(\frac{P_a}{P_b}\right) \left(\frac{D_b}{D_a}\right)^3 \dots\dots\dots\dots\dots\dots\dots\dots\dots \textbf{(4)}$$

$$D_b = \frac{D_a + D_b}{1 + 3\sqrt{\frac{P_a}{P_b}}} \dots\dots\dots\dots\dots\dots\dots\dots\dots \textbf{(5)}$$

These formulas are intended to be used for the same purposes as are formulas (1) and (2), except that they are to be used in studying the movement of retail trade between a small town and a large metropolitan center. Converse regards (4) and (5) as tentative because "we do not have enough data as yet to measure the accuracy of this adjustment."[20]

The final formula developed by Converse, formula (6), represents a modification of formula (3). Converse found that because of congestion and parking difficulties in Chicago, neighboring small towns retain a larger proportion of their fashion goods trade than is average for towns in Illinois. Using data reflecting this fact, Converse determined that the average inertia-distance factor for towns in the vicinity of Chicago was 1.5. He, therefore, modified formula (3) as follows:

[20]Converse, *op. cit.*, p. 383.

$$\frac{B_a}{B_b} = \left(\frac{P_a}{P_b}\right) \left(\frac{1.5}{d}\right)^2 \quad \cdots\cdots\cdots\cdots\cdots\cdots\cdots (6)$$

This formula can be used in the same way as formula (3), but it is applicable to the study of the movement of fashion goods trade between a small town in the vicinity of Chicago and Chicago.

Methodology Used to Develop the Laws of Retail Gravitation

The method used to develop Reilly's law is an example of the use of regression analysis to discover a scientific law. In this instance the division of retail trade between two cities is taken as the dependent variable, and population and distance are taken as independent variables.[21]

As regards his use of these two specific factors as independent variables, Reilly asserts:

> It is so readily acceptable that the amount of outside trade which a city enjoys in any surrounding town is a direct function of the population of that city and an inverse function of the distance of the city from that town, that the general law[22] needs no support.[23]

Reilly uses distance as an inverse independent variable because it is inconvenient and costly for purchasers to travel to shop. When he uses population as a direct independent variable, Reilly does not mean to

---

[21] Reilly's law can be converted to the more familiar form of a regression equation as follows:

1. $\dfrac{B_a}{B_b} = \left(\dfrac{P_a}{P_b}\right) \left(\dfrac{D_b}{D_a}\right)^2$

2. $R = X\,(Y)^2$

    where $R = \dfrac{B_a}{B_b};\ X = \dfrac{P_a}{P_b};\ Y = \dfrac{D_b}{D_a}$

If equation (2) is converted to a logarithmic form one obtains:

3. $\log R = 0 + 1 \log X + 2 \log y$

[22] $\dfrac{B_a}{B_b} = \left(\dfrac{P_a}{P_b}\right)^N \left(\dfrac{D_b}{D_a}\right)^n$

[23] Reilly, *The Law of Retail Gravitation*, p. 71.

say that it is the fact of a large cluster of people alone which causes purchasers to travel to a large city to shop. He asserts that it is the existence of such attractions as large retail stores with a wide variety of goods, social and amusement attractions, and advertising media in the large city which cause people to buy in the city. But, Reilly writes, the existence of such establishments would not be economically feasible in the absence of a relatively large population. Thus, he believes that there is a direct relationship between the factors which induce or enable individuals to travel to a city to shop and the size of that city's population.[24] In view of this relationship, Reilly considers that it aids prediction to use population as a proxy variable for these other factors.[25]

Reilly sums up the basis for his use of population and distance as the independent variables in his law as follows:

> In other words, the evidence secured in our national study[26] shows that the *population* of a city and the *distance* from that city to another comparable city are the primary factors that condition the retail trade influence of that city; that population and distance are reliable indexes of the behavior of other factors; that other factors are either so closely related to, or so directly dependent upon, these two primary factors that the effects of the dependent factors tend to balance out when cities are compared on the basis of population and distance.[27]

In view of these considerations Reilly accepts the general equation:

$$\frac{B_a}{B_b} = \left(\frac{P_a}{P_b}\right)^N \left(\frac{D_b}{D_a}\right)^n$$

and states that his problem is to find appropriate values for the exponents N and n. The value of N is determined to be 1 on the basis

[24]In constructing a market area map for shopping goods some years ago, the Research Department of the Curtis Publishing Company concluded that substitution of "shopping line sales" in place of population in Reilly's formula yielded more accurate results. See Frank Strohkarck and Katherine Phelps, "The Mechanics of Constructing a Market Area Map," *Journal of Marketing*, national quarterly publication of the American Marketing Association, Vol. XII (April, 1948), pp. 495–96.

[25]Reilly, *op. cit.*, pp. 30–32. In this same source, pp. 73–75, Reilly "ventures" a provisional list, ". . . of factors that *may* affect the retail trade influence of any given city." His list includes the following factors: lines of transportation, lines of communication, class of consumer in the territory surrounding the market, proximity of the market to a larger-city market, business attractions of the city, social and amusement attractions of the city, locations of parking facilities and railway stations in relation to business and amusement centers, nature of competition offered by smaller cities and towns in the surrounding territory, population of the city, distance which prospective customers must travel in order to reach the city, and the psychology of distance prevailing in that part of the country, the topographical and climatic conditions peculiar to the city and its surrounding territory, and the kind of leadership offered by the owners or managers of various business interests of the city.

[26]Reilly does not present this evidence.

[27]Reilly, *op. cit.* pp. 31–32.

of certain of his studies.   While he does not present these studies, he
states that they show that the outside trade enjoyed by different-sized
cities and towns indicate that a city with twice the population of
another adjacent city enjoys about twice as much outside retail business
in the territory between two cities and that a city five times the population of another adjacent city enjoys about five times as much outside
trade in the intermediate territory.   "In other words," Reilly writes,
"by personal investigation we have approximated the *rate* at which
outside trade drawn by a city increases with the population of that
city, and we have evidence to support the use of the first power of the
population, i.e., 'N' equals 1."[28]

In order to find the value of n Reilly starts with the equation:

1. $$\frac{B_a}{B_b} = \left(\frac{P_a}{P_b}\right)^N \left(\frac{D_b}{D_a}\right)^n$$

Substituting 1 for N he obtains

2. $$\frac{B_a}{B_b} = \left(\frac{P_a}{P_b}\right) \left(\frac{D_b}{D_a}\right)^n$$

He then solves for n as follows:

3. $$\left(\frac{D_b}{D_a}\right)^n = \left(\frac{B_a}{B_b}\right) \left(\frac{P_b}{P_a}\right)$$

4. $$n \log \left(\frac{D_b}{D_a}\right) = \log \left(\frac{B_a}{B_b} \times \frac{P_b}{P_a}\right)$$

5. $$n = \frac{\log \left(\dfrac{B_a}{B_b} \times \dfrac{P_b}{P_a}\right)}{\log \left(\dfrac{D_b}{D_a}\right)}$$

In solving for n in equation (5), as an empirical formula, Reilly
had to obtain values for the unknowns on the right-hand side of this
equation.   Since in any one case he was studying the retail trade
influence of two specific trading centers on intermediate towns, he
obtained population data for the relevant trading centers, i.e., values

---

[28]*Ibid.*, pp. 71–72.

for P_a and P_b.[29] In obtaining the appropriate values for equation (5), Reilly restricted himself to those intermediate towns which constituted breaking points between any two pair of trading centers. Since at a breaking point town $B_a/B_b = 1$, his remaining problem was to find the breaking point town between two trading centers and then measure the distance between this town and the relevant trading centers, i.e., D_b and D_a. To solve this problem Reilly states:

> We drove along the main automobile highways connecting larger cities and called upon the secretary of the Retail Credit Men's Association in intermediate cities and towns.[30] On the basis of the records of credit inquiries kept in these offices, we were able to find that point at which the preponderance of retail trade ceased to flow in the direction of the city we had left and began to flow in the direction of the city we were approaching.[31]

When the breaking point town was determined in this manner, Reilly could ascertain D_b and D_a by consulting a highway map of the area. After obtaining values for P_a, P_b, D_b, and D_a in this manner, Reilly solved for n in 255 cases and obtained the following frequency distribution:

Value of n	No. of Cases
0.00 – 1.5	45
1.51 – 2.5	87
2.51 – 3.5	35
3.51 – 4.5	24
4.51 – 5.5	15
5.51 – 6.5	14
6.51 – 7.5	6
7.51 – 8.5	5
8.51 – 9.5	12
9.51 – 10.5	5
10.51 – 11.5	3
11.51 – 12.5	4

---

[29]In the areas studied by Reilly, the larger cities to which trade flowed from intermediate towns were designated as retail trading centers.

[30]Reilly conducted his investigation during the period 1927–30. He studied the division of trade among competing retail trade centers in the following states: Alabama, New York, Georgia, Texas, Maryland, Illinois, Massachusetts, Connecticut, Virginia, Indiana, Missouri, Tennessee, Ohio, Pennsylvania, Florida, Louisiana, Kentucky, Oregon, Minnesota, Washington, and the District of Columbia.

[31]Reilly, *The Law of Retail Gravitation*, p. 64.

On the basis of this distribution Reilly concluded: "In other words, a clear mode occurs in the range of 1.51–2.5 which shows that the exponent of the distance is nearer to the second power than to any other even power."[32] That is, $n = 2$.

Formula (3), $\dfrac{B_a}{B_b} = \left(\dfrac{P_a}{H_b}\right)\left(\dfrac{4}{d}\right)^2$

also has its origin in Reilly's original law. Converse started with the equation $\dfrac{B_a}{B_b} = \left(\dfrac{P_a}{P_b}\right)\left(\dfrac{D_b}{D_a}\right)^2$.

Town B in this formula was designated the home town. P_a and P_b are population values which can be obtained from census data or can be estimated. D_a is the distance from the home town to the outside town. B_a was designated the percentage of the home town's total fashion goods purchases made in town A, and B_b was designated as the proportion of the home town's total fashion goods retained. Converse and his staff conducted consumer surveys in more than 100 towns, and on the basis of these surveys he obtained the values for B_a and B_b.[33] He then solved Reilly's original equation for D_b in 100 cases, obtaining an arithmetic mean of 4.5 miles and a median of 3.9 miles.[34] On the basis of these findings Converse decided to use 4 as the inertia-distance factor. This factor reflects the inertia that must be overcome to visit a store even a block away.

Formula (4) $\dfrac{B_a}{B_b} = \left(\dfrac{P_a}{P_b}\right)\left(\dfrac{D_b}{D_a}\right)^3$

is intended to be used in situations where the population of the trading center is more than 20 times the size of the intermediate town. Converse tentatively presents this modification,[35] i.e., use of the cube of the distances rather than their square, because, as of 1949, he did not yet have enough data to measure the accuracy of this adjustment.

Converse has not published the data on which this modification is based. However, it apparently stems from his study of the movement of shopping goods trade to Chicago and St. Louis from towns in the vicinity of the breaking points of the trading territories of these cities. He apparently found that, in this type of situation, use of the cube of

---

[32]William J. Reilly, *Methods for the Study of Retail Relationships* (Austin: University of Texas Press, 1929), p. 50.

[33]Converse, "New Laws of Retail Gravitation," p. 380.

[34]*Ibid.*, pp. 380–381.

[35]*Ibid.*, p. 383.

the distances increased predictive accuracy. However, the data available to him at the time did not permit him to measure the accuracy of the adjustment. Converse speculates that the necessity for this adjustment probably stems from the trade-repelling effect of traffic congestion and parking difficulties in large towns.

Formula (5) Breaking point, distance from B $=$

$$\frac{Distance\ between\ towns\ A\ and\ B}{1\ +\ \sqrt[3]{\dfrac{Population\ of\ town\ A}{Population\ of\ town\ B}}}$$

can be derived from formula (4) in the same way that formula (2) was derived from formula (1).[36]

In formula (6) $\quad \dfrac{B_a}{B_b} = \left(\dfrac{P_a}{H_b}\right)\left(\dfrac{1.5}{d}\right)^2$

Converse uses an average inertia factor of 1.5 rather than 4 as is the case in formula (3). Formula (6) is recommended for use in studying the division of fashion goods trade from small towns in the vicinity of Chicago, to Chicago.

To obtain an average inertia factor of 1.5, Converse studied the division of fashion goods trade from 13 towns to Chicago. As was the case with formula (3) (see p. 20 of this study), Converse determined the values of B_a and B_b from consumer surveys.[37] He then solved for the numerator of the distance ratio and obtained an arithmetic mean and median equal to 1.5. Converse conjectures that for towns in the vicinity of Chicago residents make more of their fashion goods purchases in their home town rather than expose themselves to the traffic congestion of Chicago.

Tests of the Laws of Retail Gravitation

To test his law Reilly took 30 pairs of trading centers and, using his formula, computed the location of the breaking point between each

---

[36]See pp. 12–13 of this study.

[37]Converse does not present the B_a and B_b values obtained through consumer surveys on the basis of which he arrived at an inertia factor of 1.5 for the 13 cities in the vicinity of Chicago that he studied. The nonavailability of these data prevents computation of a measure reflecting the extent of agreement between the B_a, B_b predictions of formula (6) and those obtained by Converse in his consumer surveys, i. e., a coefficient of determination. See Converse, "New Laws of Retail Gravitation," pp. 383–84.

pair of cities.[38]   He then conducted field studies to determine the location of the breaking point towns between each of the 30 pairs of cities.

---

[38]This can be done as follows. Starting with the law of retail gravitation:

1. $\dfrac{B_a}{B_b} = \left(\dfrac{P_a}{P_b}\right) \left(\dfrac{D_b}{D_a}\right)^2$

1 can be substituted for B_a/B_b because, by definition, a breaking point town is one from which two competing centers equally divide the retail trade that leaves the town for these two trading centers.

2. $1 = \left(\dfrac{P_a}{P_b}\right) \left(\dfrac{D_b}{D_a}\right)^2$

Solving for D_b/D_a we obtain:

$$\left(\dfrac{D_b}{D_a}\right)^2 = \dfrac{P_b}{P_a}$$

$$\dfrac{D_b}{D_a} = \sqrt{\dfrac{P_b}{P_a}}$$

Using census data or estimates of the population of the two relevant trading centers, a value for D_b/D_a can be obtained. Since the value for $D_b + D_a$ can be determined, i.e., the distance between the two trading centers on the best road connecting these two cities, one can solve for D_b and D_a. Suppose that the calculations give a value for $D_b/D_a = 2$. Then the following operations can be performed:

$$\dfrac{D_b}{D_a} = 2$$

$$D_b + D_a = 150$$

$$D_b = 150 - D_a$$

$$\dfrac{150 - D_a}{D_a} = 2$$

$$150 - D_a = 2\,D_a$$

$$150 = 3\,D_a$$

$$D_a = 50$$

$$\text{Since } D_b + D_a = 150$$

$$D_b + 50 \; = 150$$

$$D_b = 100$$

That is, by use of Reilly's formula it has been predicted that the breaking point town located on the best road between city A and city B is 50 miles from city A and 100 miles from city B.

A comparison of the locations predicted by the law with those yielded by the field studies is presented in the following table:

Table I

**LOCATION OF BREAKING POINT TOWNS FOR A
NATIONAL SAMPLE OF RETAIL TRADING CENTERS**

Breaking Point Town	Reilly's Law Prediction[39] (miles)	Field Study Results[39] (miles)
Collier, Georgia	66	64
Heflin, Alabama	89	87
Salada, Texas	55	55
Westfield, New York	60	58
Elkmont Springs, Tennessee	128	127
Springfield, Illinois	204	202
Middletown, Ohio	39	38
Northeast, Pennsylvania	109	113
East Springfield, Pennsylvania	76	80
Harmony, Ohio	37	38
Hillsbury, Texas	73	70
Midway between Tyler & Longview, Texas	139	133
Meriden, Connecticut	19	18
Midway between Giddings & Ledbetter, Texas	110	101
Devers, Texas	63	60
Schulenberg, Texas	114	109
Centerville, Indiana	61	62
Mt. Etna, Indiana	77	85
Uniontown, Indiana	62	74
Fender, Georgia	169	160
Chilhowie, Virginia	161	157
Kingsburg, California	223	215
Midway between Ocean Springs and Pascagoula, Mississippi	118	113
Palmer, Massachusetts	149	151
Meadville, Pennsylvania	111	110
Tipton, Missouri	169	171
Midway between Sinton and Skidmore, Texas	115	116
Midway between Kyle & San Marcos, Texas	58	55
Chehalis, Washington	102	101
Midway between Fredericksburg and Galansville, Virginia	71	69

Source: W. J. Reilly, *The Law of Retail Gravitation* (1st ed.; New York: William J. Reilly Company, 1931), pp. 25–29.

[39]The distances presented in these columns are from the same city in each pair of trading centers studied.

After comparing the data in the second and third columns of Table I, Reilly concluded that his law was "startlingly" accurate.

In 1943 Converse published a study in which he revealed the results of his efforts to check the accuracy of Reilly's law.[40] His study compared the predictions of Reilly's law with the movement of retail trade ascertained through consumer surveys.

Converse focused on the retail trading area of Champaign-Urbana, Illinois.   Nearby primary trading centers[41] which compete with Champaign-Urbana for the retail trade of intermediate towns are given as Bloomington, Danville, Kankakee, and Mattoon.   Thirteen towns located between Champaign-Urbana and the five primary trading centers were studied.[42]   For each of these towns Converse predicted the relative division of the retail trade which left the town for Champaign-Urbana and a competing city, using Reilly's law. Converse regarded these data as reflecting the division of shopping goods purchases between two cities.

By means of consumer surveys, he then determined how many families in the towns studied made their shopping goods purchases in nearby primary trading centers. With this information he computed the percentages of consumers who bought shopping goods in Champaign-Urbana and the competing trading centers.   He then calculated a coefficient of correlation between the predictions made by Reilly's law and the percentages computed on the basis of the survey information collected in 11 of the 13 towns. He obtained a coefficient of +.88 and concluded that "on the whole, it (Reilly's law) works with a relatively high degree of accuracy."[43]

In a later publication Converse reported that he had subjected Reilly's law to an additional test. For nine of the towns included in the study discussed above, and two additional ones, Converse estimated the dollar amounts spent on fashion goods by the inhabitants of each town in nearby trading centers. On the basis of these estimates he calculated the percentage division of fashion goods trade leaving each town for the relevant pair of competing trading centers. He then computed the coefficient of correlation between these percentages and those

---

[40]Converse, *A Study of Retail Trade Areas in East Central Illinois*, pp. 23–54.

[41]Converse defined a primary trading center in this study as a town of more than 10,000 population.

[42]Onarga, Buckley, Cissna Park, Ogden, Fithian, Homer, Tuscola, Arcola, Monticello, Deland, Farmer City, Bement, and Gibson City.

[43]See Converse, *A Study of Retail Trade Areas in East Central Illinois*, pp. 44–48.

predicted by the law of retail gravitation. His calculations yielded a coefficient of +.93.[44]

This result reinforced Converse's confidence in the predictive accuracy of Reilly's law which had been based on his earlier computation of a coefficient of correlation of +.88. Despite this confidence he added the following caution:

> It should not, however, be concluded that the law will measure the movement of trade with such accuracy in all territories. The towns included in the computations used here are in a territory in which the primary trading centers are considerably larger than the intermediate towns. In areas where there is less difference in size between the primary and secondary trading centers or between the trading centers and the towns from which they draw trade, the law of retail gravitation may perhaps not predict the movement of trade with the accuracy found in the territory here studied.[45]

Converse's experience with Reilly's law has led him to place the following limitations on its use:

1. The law of retail gravitation applies only to towns in the vicinity of the breaking points between two large towns.
2. Reilly's law applies only to the delineation of trading areas for shopping goods and particularly to fashion goods, sometimes referred to as "style" or "specialty" goods. This is so because a considerable part of convenience and bulk goods is purchased locally.[46]

Another test of the law of retail gravitation was conducted by Robert Reynolds.[47] Using data describing the movement of retail trade in Iowa in 1935 and 1949, Reynolds sought to determine whether formula (2), the breaking point formula, can "safely" be used to locate the breaking point between two trading areas.

---

[44]Paul D. Converse, *Retail Trade Areas in Illinois* (Urbana: University of Illinois Press, 1946), pp. 13 and 18.

[45]*Ibid.*, p. 18.

[46]*Ibid.*, p. 26. Converse defines shopping goods as those that have great importance attached to them by those who purchase them. They are usually goods of large unit value, goods which are important in the family budget. Many of them are purchased at infrequent intervals, and the purchases are usually planned long in advance.

In the purchase of fashion goods, according to Converse, the typical consumer wants something distinctive, something to suit a specific need or individual taste. In the search for fashion newness, consumers may visit several stores and are willing to travel considerable distances to reach stores with stocks large enough to give them large assortments from which to choose.

Converse defines bulk goods as goods of such weight or bulk that delivery accounts for an important part of the cost. Bulk goods are usually purchased near home, largely because of the cost of delivery, and are often purchased over the telephone. The most important bulk goods are building materials, coal, fuel, oil, and feeds.

[47]Robert B. Reynolds, "A Test of the Law of Retail Gravitation," *Journal of Marketing*, national quarterly publication of the American Marketing Association, Vol. XVII (January, 1953), pp. 273–277.

In order to test formula (2), Reynolds took the logarithmic expression of a generalized version of this formula,[48]

$$n = \frac{log\left(\dfrac{P_b}{P_a}\right)}{log\left(\dfrac{D_b}{D_a}\right)}$$

and sought to determine whether n differed significantly from formula (2). Using a quota sample of data collected in 1935 for 91 Iowa counties and data collected in 1949 for Southwest Iowa, Reynolds computed regression equations for groceries, eggs and poultry, movies, farm machinery, lumber and cement, physicians' services, women's coats and dresses, men's good shoes, and men's suits.[49]

The data Reynolds had available to him described the trading areas of specific trading centers for each of these products. Reynolds describes his study as follows:

> From . . . [the] . . . points, where trading area boundaries crossed roads, highway distances to the nearest mile (D_1 and D_2) were measured to the two trading centers in question and the populations of the centers (P_1 and P_2) were recorded to the nearest hundred. Two values each of D (D_1/D_2 and D_2/D_1) and P (P_1/P_2 and P_2/P_1) then were computed for every breaking point.

> Values of P and D were plotted graphically before starting the analysis in order to determine whether some curve other than the theoretical power function might fit the data better. No such curve was found; so it became necessary to rectify the data by taking logarithms of P and D before proceeding with the usual least-squares solution. In short, the problem resolved itself to finding the value of the constant, b, in the following linear equation, . . .: $log \, D = b \, log \, P$.[50]

---

[48]A general form of formula (2) can be written as follows:

$$1 = \left(\frac{P_a}{P_b}\right)\left(\frac{D_b}{D_a}\right)^n$$

[49]This list contains services, convenience goods, and industrial materials, as well as shopping goods. Since formula (2) is supposed to hold only for shopping goods, Reynolds' test was appropriate only with respect to women's coats and dresses, men's suits, and men's good shoes.

[50]In this equation:

$$D = D_b/D_a$$
$$P = P_b/P_a$$
$$b = 1/n$$

This b is the exponent of P in Converse's formula, where it is .50, or the square root.[51]

In addition to calculating a b value for each of the commodities he studied, Reynolds also computed coefficients of determination for these products. His computations are shown in Table II.

Table II

**REYNOLDS' TEST OF REILLY'S LAW —
VALUES OF b AND r^2 (1935 AND 1949*)**

Product	1935		1949*	
	b	r^2	b	r^2
Groceries	.31	.68	.46	.71
Eggs and Poultry, marketing of	.32	.68	.17**	.12**
Movies	.31	.59	.38	.48
Lumber and Cement	.22	.58	n.s.	n.s.
Farm Machinery	n.s.	n.s.	.51	.63
Physician	.22	.43	.27	.24
Women's Coats & Dresses	.44	.79	.51***	.90***
Men's Suits	.45	.76	n.s.	n.s.
Men's Good Shoes	n.s.	n.s.	.50	.75

* Southwest Iowa only.
** Eggs only.
*** Women's Coats only.
n.s.: Not studied.

Source: Robert B. Reynolds, "A Test of the Law of Retail Gravitation," *Journal of Marketing*, national quarterly publication of the American Marketing Association, Vol. XVII (January, 1953), pp. 275–276.

In Table II a b value equal to .50 means that the breaking points predicted by formula (2) agree exactly with those revealed by Reynolds' survey data. Reynolds tested the significance of the difference between each b value and .50 to determine whether the differences were due to chance or were probably significant. Reynolds found that for 1935 the differences were significant and concluded that these data constituted evidence warranting a rejection of formula (2).

A similar test performed for the 1949 b values produced significant differences for the products studied with the exception of the shopping goods items (women's coats and dresses, and men's suits), and Reynolds concluded that insofar as shopping goods were concerned the 1949 data did not contribute to a rejection of formula (2).

[51]Reynolds, *op. cit.*, p. 275.

Reynolds also computed coefficients of determination in order to ascertain the extent to which the variation in the location of breaking point towns between trading centers was "explained" by reference to the population of the relevant trading centers. For the shopping goods he studied, Reynolds found that these coefficients fell within the range of .75–.90.[52]

In the October 1959 issue of the *Journal of Marketing*, A. F. Jung presented some data which, he maintains, contradict Reilly's law. Jung wrote that a study of the buying habits of the residents of Columbia, Missouri showed no preference for patronizing the merchants of St. Louis rather than those of Kansas City. According to Reilly's law, Jung states, Columbia residents should have favored the St. Louis merchants by a substantial margin.[53] Reilly has countered by arguing that Jung has not invalidated his *general* law. The most Jung does, according to Reilly, is to invalidate a judgment that $N = 1$ and $n = 2$ as regards the pulls of St. Louis and Kansas City on Columbia.[54]

Jung's position is based on his finding that:

> There was no significant difference between the number of shopping trips (for ladies' ready-to-wear) to Kansas City and St. Louis, even though St. Louis has almost twice the population of Kansas City, and is six miles closer to Columbia (125 miles distant as compared with 131 miles).[55]

Strictly speaking Jung, in order to support his conclusion, needed to collect data on the *volume* of ladies' ready-to-wear sales going to Kansas City and St. Louis from Columbia. However, even if Jung's finding

---

[52]See Robert B. Reynolds, "A Test of the Law of Retail Gravitation," *Journal of Marketing* (January, 1953), pp. 275–276. After the publication of Reynolds' findings, Converse commented on the study and was answered by Reynolds. See Robert B. Reynolds, "Rejoinder to Converse's Comment on Reynolds' Test of the Law of Retail Gravitation," *Journal of Marketing*, national quarterly publication of the American Marketing Association, Vol. XVIII (October, 1953), pp. 170–174. This discussion reflected a lack of communication between the two participants and did not shed much light on the validity of formula (2). Examples of this lack of communication are: (a) Converse maintains that Reynolds did not state his methods. Reynolds says that he did. (b) Reynolds used statistical methods to test the accuracy of formula (2) while Converse used subjective judgment. (c) Reynolds' apparent unfamiliarity with Converse's concept of a primary trading center was the basis for some confusion in the discussion. (d) In Reynolds' view, even if formula (2) possessed "good" predictive accuracy, it could not be expected to predict accurately in any one specific application. Rather, the formula's accuracy would be manifested when used to predict many breaking points. In contrast, Converse apparently expects formula (2) to predict accurately in specific instances.

[53]A. F. Jung, "Is Reilly's Law of Retail Gravitation Always True," *Journal of Marketing*, national quarterly publication of the American Marketing Association, Vol. XXIV (October, 1959), pp. 62–63.

[54]Reilly stated this position at the Illinois Symposium in October, 1959.

[55]Jung, *op. cit.*, p. 62.

can be said to contradict Reilly's formula, it cannot be concluded that it invalidates the formula. The formula is supposed to be accurate *on the average*. The fact that its prediction and fact do not precisely agree in any one instance does not necessarily invalidate Reilly's formula.

Evaluation of the Laws of Retail Gravitation

In his several studies, Reilly set as his objective the discovery of some methods for measuring the retail trade influence of a city. For his part, Converse has focused on refining the results of Reilly's studies and developing new measures of the movement of retail trade among cities.

The essence of the contributions by Reilly and Converse is represented by the six equations which are termed the laws of retail gravitation. Each of these equations has been explained in preceding pages. It has been pointed out that neither Reilly nor Converse assert that the laws will predict accurately in every instance. They do, however, hold that the equations give usefully accurate predictions for either the United States or Illinois.

These several laws of retail gravitation are based to a large extent on Reilly's original formula.[56] In this formula the division of the outgoing retail trade of an intermediate town between two competing trading centers is made directly dependent on the population of the two competing trading centers and inversely dependent upon some power of the distance between the intermediate town and the respective trading centers. Population is used as a proxy variable for a number of factors[57] which Reilly asserts attract residents of small towns to nearby trading centers. Reilly, moreover, asserts that the division of retail trade between two trading centers varies directly with their population in a 1 : 1 ratio.

That such factors as large department stores, social and amusement attractions, and advertising media in a city attract buyers to that trading center is widely supported by marketing literature. However,

---

[56]Although Reilly makes no reference to Newton's Law of Gravitation, the similarity between Newton's Law and his is noteworthy. The two are similar in that Reilly uses business volume instead of force, population instead of mass, with distance remaining unchanged. John Q. Stewart writes that Reilly's law is derivable from Newton's Law of Gravitation and thinks that it represents the first recognition of demographic gravitation. See J. Q. Stewart, "Demographic Gravitation: Evidence and Applications," *Sociometry* (February–May, 1948), p. 35.

[57]See pp. 16–17 of this study.

in order to justify his use of population as a proxy variable for such trade attracting factors, Reilly needed to demonstrate that the existence of these factors varies directly with population with a coefficient of correlation of $+1$. This, of course, would be difficult to demonstrate, if it could be demonstrated at all. Moreover, Reilly does not present data supporting his use of a 1 : 1 relationship between business volume and population when D_a and D_b are not equal.

Reilly does present data supporting his use of an inverse relationship between business volume and distance.[58] His use of an exponent of 2 for the distance ratio is obtained by an appropriate use of frequency distribution analysis. However, it is not known whether the sample from which he obtained his data is representative of United States trading centers because it is not a random probability sample.

Thus, while the structure of formulas (1) and (2) has considerable marketing plausibility, the difficulty and expense of providing the necessary statistical substantiation are of such apparent magnitude that it is understandable that these have not been provided by Reilly and Converse. However, it needs to be noted that the absence of such statistical substantiation raises questions as to the validity of formulas (1) and (2) and the related formulas developed subsequently.

Even in the absence of this substantiating information, though, it may be possible, through use, to demonstrate that the formulas give acceptably accurate predictions. The tests made by Reilly, Converse, and Reynolds do not provide evidence for a rejection of formulas (1) and (2). Reilly's conclusion that his law was "startlingly" accurate was based on his examination of the absolute deviations between the predictions of his law and the information gained from his consumer surveys. These deviations, in his view, were small enough to justify his conclusion.

If Reilly's test data are subjected to further analysis, it is seen that the law did, in fact, provide quite accurate predictions for the sample of trading centers included in his study. However, the sample predictions reflect an upward bias in the law.

For purposes of this evaluation, Reilly's test data (see Table I, p. 23) have been plotted in Figure 1. A least squares regression line has been fitted to the data, and it is shown as AB. The equation describing this line is:

---

[58]Reilly, *Methods for the Study of Retail Relationships*, p. 28.

$$Y_c = 1.87 + .97X$$

where X represents the breaking point predictions resulting from the use of Reilly's law.

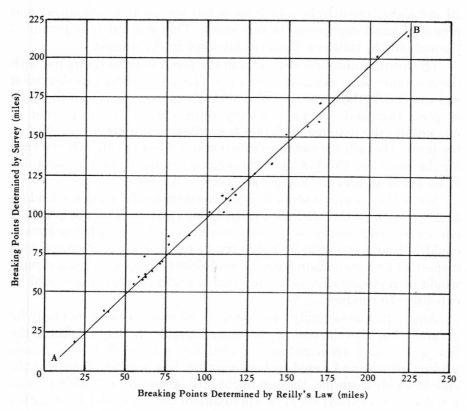

Figure 1

**LOCATION OF BREAKING POINT TOWNS
FOR A NATIONAL SAMPLE OF RETAIL TRADING CENTERS**

The data yield a coefficient of determination of .98. This means that 98 per cent of the variation in the breaking point distances revealed by consumer surveys is explained by reference to Reilly's law. If the coefficient of determination had turned out to be 1.00, all the points in Figure 1 would lie on AB. If this had been the case, it would mean that the breaking point distances predicted by Reilly's law would agree exactly with those determined by consumer survey.

An upward bias in the sample predictions is revealed by further analysis of Reilly's test data. These data show that the law yielded predictions which were higher than the consumer survey results in 20 instances, predictions which were too low in nine instances, and produced exact agreement in one case. This upward bias prevailed throughout the range of distances involved in the sample.

The average absolute deviation in the predictions as compared with the consumer surveys was 3.53 miles.[59] The average absolute deviation was smallest in the lower one third of the distances. That is, if the pairs of prediction and consumer survey data are arrayed according to magnitude, the average deviation is smallest in the lower one third of the pairs. Overall, the average deviation was 3.5 per cent. The average for the lower one third of the data is 3.2 per cent, the middle one third is 4.7 per cent, and the highest one third is 2.7 per cent.

While the various tests of Reilly's law do not offer evidence leading to a rejection of the law, the available information does not permit a conclusive judgment as to the law's accuracy. Before such a judgment could be made, it would be necessary to test the law's accuracy with respect to an appropriate national probability sample. Such a sample would be representative of United States trading centers but would be expensive to conduct.

Any appraisal of Reilly's law needs to take into account not only its accuracy but also the cost of consumer surveys. It may be that if the law were tested on a national probability sample of United States trading centers and found to be somewhat less accurate than was the case in Reilly's sample, the law might still be useful to shopping goods retailers if it enabled them to approximate certain useful information without incurring the cost of expensive consumer surveys.

An evaluation of formula (3), which is related to Reilly's law, raises much the same issues as were raised in connection with the evaluation of formulas (1) and (2). For example, Converse does not support his use of a 1 : 1 relationship between the division of trade and the populations of the home town and the nearby trading center.

---

[59]This average was calculated as follows: The consumer survey results were subtracted from the relevant predictions made by use of Reilly's formula. Ignoring negative signs, these data were then totaled and the sum was divided by the number of items. The measure—3.5 miles—states the average deviation of the Reilly formula predictions from the breaking points determined by consumer survey.

Moreover, the sample, on the basis of which an inertia-distance factor of 4 was obtained, consisted of Illinois towns and is not claimed to be representative of United States towns and trading centers. All that can be said for formula (3) is that it may hold for Illinois. Whether it can be used as a predictive device elsewhere is not known.

As for formulas (4), (5), and (6), these are presented by Converse only as tentative formulations. They are based on small samples and have not been tested extensively. For this reason no evaluatory comment is presented here with respect to these formulas.

While Converse emphasizes the predictive accuracy of formulas (1)–(6), he also points up the fact that these formulas enable retail merchants to compute averages useful to them. The averages provided by the laws of retail gravitation could be used, according to him, in much the same way that average cost information provided by trade associations is used.

For example, shopping goods merchants in city A could locate the breaking point town between city A and city B by use of formula (2). Then, by means of a consumer survey they could determine whether the outgoing shopping goods trade was, in fact, equally divided between city A and city B. If city A was getting less than 50 per cent of this trade, the merchants could conclude that their business volume was below average in this respect. On the basis of this information they might wish to take promotional action aimed at bringing the inflow of shopping goods trade at least up to the average.

Whether the laws of retail gravitation can be used in the manner suggested by Converse depends on their predictive accuracy when applied to various parts of the United States. If they typically predict with substantial accuracy, then Converse's suggestion is useful.

By way of summary, it can be said that the available information does not offer evidence for a rejection of Reilly's law and of the related formulas developed by Converse. For reasons stated above in this evaluation, however, it is uncertain whether the formulas can yet be regarded as marketing laws.[60] Although it cannot yet be said that Reilly and Converse have attained their objective of discovering a method for measuring the retail trade influence of a city, the results of future work

---

[60]In the preface to the second edition of *The Law of Retail Gravitation* (p. iii) published in 1953, Reilly writes: "For those who wonder whether the law of retail gravitation, first stated over twenty years ago, still holds, it may be reassuring that large organizations with competent research staffs are currently using the law and find it as

in this area may provide the basis for a conclusive evaluation of their contribution to marketing theory.

---

sound as ever." Unfortunately, Reilly does not publish the information on which he bases this statement.

The manuscript of this chapter was sent to Professor Converse prior to publication. He made the following comments.

There were several [other] studies, not mentioned, published at the University of Illinois, relating to the law of retail gravitation, by Dave Luck, George Martin, myself, and others. Most of these were published by the Bureau of Business Research or its successor the Bureau of Economic and Business Research. Some were published by the Bureau of Business Management. These included East Central Illinois, South Central Illinois, Rockford, Kankakee, Crab Orchard, Bloomington, Hoopeston, Waukegan, Englewood, and some others.

In the Englewood Study Martin found that the law of retail gravitation applied reasonably well within a large city, Chicago, by using time on street cars or busses. Studies made in various European countries used time or cost on public carriers for miles.

A study by Victor Bennett of Laurel, Maryland, a town midway between two large cities is a very interesting study (Victor Bennett, "Consumer Buying Habits in a Small Town Located Between Two Large Cities," *Journal of Marketing*, April 1944, pp. 405–16).

In the study by Curtis Publishing Company, Donald Hobart used fashion goods sales instead of population. This appears good if the object is to state what the situation is, rather than what it should be. One use of the studies is to point out to the merchants of a town what they are doing — average, better than average, or poorer than average (Reilly's law prediction=average performance). In some studies for planned shopping centers, square feet devoted to the sale of fashion goods are substituted for population figures. See, for example, studies of Harry J. Casey, *Broadening Perspectives of Marketing*, 1956, published by the American Marketing Association.

My suggestion for using the cube of the distance for comparing a large city with a much smaller city is only a suggestion for further study.

I have had students make studies of retail trade areas located all over the United States — computing income of area, boundaries of trade areas by Reilly's Law, proportion of trade done in the shopping centers, etc. In practically every case results were as expected. Of course "common sense" must be used. For example, the population of a town increases, or new highways shorten distances, and retail stores lag in increasing their stocks. How long does it take to adjust to changes in population or highway distances?

We need more studies of trade movements within metropolitan areas and in the sparsely populated high plains and arid regions of the country. There is plenty of room for study. For example, how has the development of planned shopping centers affected the movement of retail trade?

An interesting study of medical trade areas was done by Dr. Frank Dickinson, Economist, of the American Medical Association.

Chapter 3

SOCIAL PHYSICS

John Q. Stewart is an astrophysicist who is now engaged in the study of social phenomena. He is the leading spokesman of a group which is attempting to contribute to the building of a science called social physics. According to Stewart:

> In its applications, social physics relates directly to the economic theory of location and to general marketing theory — for example, to the construction of maps of trading centers. . . . the general possibilities of its (social physics) usefulness extend over the entire field of social statistics wherever averages rather than individual human characteristics, are studied.[1]

The Social Physics Approach to Theory

Stewart estimates the present state of social studies as little superior to that of physics at the time of the sixteenth century when physics learned to supplement words with numbers. In his evaluation of social studies he is particularly critical of deductive systems in social science because he believes that builders of such systems start with introspection and take their own actual or possible personal motives as a model for a standard man. The greatest fallacy of such deductive systems, he writes, is that they attribute to many men the characteristics which have been assumed for one standard man. The false equation, he states, that one million equals one is the extent of the mathematical reasoning of many reverently quoted authorities.[2]

Stewart also has reservations about the contributions of statisticians. He writes:

> Mathematical statisticians have seldom blazed the difficult trail which leads from observations of the world to new branches of science. Their convention-bound methods come into play only after discovery

---

[1]John Q. Stewart, "Potential of Population and Its Relationship to Marketing," published in Reavis Cox and Wroe Alderson (eds.), *Theory in Marketing* (Homewood, Illinois: Richard D. Irwin, 1950), p. 19.

[2]John Q. Stewart, "A Basis for Social Physics," *Impact of Science on Society* (Summer, 1952), p. 122.

of the leading concepts and relations of the new field. Statistics necessarily is microscopic. It deals with the data of special cases and can work with broad data only if the cases already have been put together by connections discovered in studies in the field in question. The operation of a principle may be obscured by the simultaneous effects of other principles, and mere statistics cannot, in complete ignorance of conditions, sort out the principles.[3]

In Stewart's view the development of science can be illustrated by the work of three astronomical investigators: Tycho Brahe (1546–1601), Johann Kepler (1571–1630), and Isaac Newton (1642–1727). Brahe accumulated many reasonably accurate observations of the position in the sky of the planets. Stewart places Brahe among the founders of modern science because precise observation was far from a routine requirement of science at the time. Kepler is also included in this category because he discovered three "laws" on the orbital motions of the planets. These are not general laws of nature, according to Stewart, but empirical statements of mathematical regularities which apply only to planetary motions. Newton is included in this triumvirate because he developed general laws of motion. Stewart writes that in developing these general laws, Newton needed only to think of Kepler's short mathematical statements instead of having to attempt the impossible task of carrying in mind many thousands of separate measurements.[4]

Social physics is defined by Stewart as including all studies of a mathematical type relating to human behavior. Social physics, he states:

> . . . analyses demographic, economic, political, and sociological situations in terms of the purely physical factors of time, distance, mass of material, and number of people with recourse also to social factors which can be shown to operate in a similar way to two other physical agents, namely temperature and electrical charge.[5]

He writes that temperature as a social factor refers to the level of activity of people, e.g., bank deposits per capita, mileage of railways

---

[3]John Q. Stewart and William Warntz, "Physics of Population Distribution," *Journal of Regional Science* (Summer, 1958), p. 118.

[4]While Stewart does not say so explicitly, he apparently makes the following distinction between an empirical regularity and a general law: Kepler's findings are regarded by Stewart as empirical regularities rather than general laws because they apply only to the orbital motions of the planets. In contrast, Newton's findings are termed general laws because they apply to matter anywhere. Stewart's distinction between an empirical regularity and a general law thus appears to hinge on the degree of generality of the findings.

[5]Stewart, "A Basis for Social Physics," p. 110.

and highways per square mile of area, and percentage of workers in manufacturing industries.[6] The social quantity that Stewart substitutes for electric charge (positive and negative) is desire. "Since desire," he writes, "in the sense of simple hunger is neutralized by its appropriate satisfaction, it is in this respect like a negative electric charge, while the desirable object possesses the neutralizing positive charge."[7] This kind of framework is termed dimensional analysis by Stewart. As applied to social physics, a principal objective of dimensional analysis is to designate the leading factors by reference to which social physics as a whole can be summarized.

The idea of social physics dates back, according to Stewart, to about 1820 when August Comte first used the term.[8] Another early student of social physics was Quetelet, the Belgian astronomer. Quetelet is said to have developed an interest in social physics in about 1835 as a result of his having become impressed by the regularity of many types of numerical social data.

The raw material of social physics is the available numerical data on society. These include such data as censuses of population, vital statistics, tables of geographic areas and distances, rents, wages, prices, public opinion polls, and psychological tests relating to social behavior. So far, Stewart writes, only a very small proportion of these data has been reduced to concise mathematical regularities.

The immediate objective of the social physicist, according to Stewart, is to discover uniformities in social behavior which can be expressed in mathematical form more or less corresponding to the known patterns of physical science. He is of the opinion that enough such regularities exist to justify the conclusion that certain types of human relations, on the average and only on the average, conform to mathematical formulas resembling the primitive "laws" of physics.

The importance that Stewart places on the collection of empirical regularities stems from his concept of the development of science, i.e., from quantifiable observations, to empirical regularities, to general laws. Collection of empirical regularities for their own sake, he writes, has often in the natural sciences been the indispensable step toward later theoretical understanding.[9]

---

[6]*Ibid.*, pp. 120–21.

[7]*Ibid.*, p. 123.

[8]There is some question as to who really originated this term and when.

[9]Stewart does not make any explicit statement as to the part that hypothesis plays in the development of scientific laws. His definition of empirical regularity (see

Social Physics : Concepts

Thus far in the development of social physics several basic concepts have been formulated which are said to constitute a rigorous set of measures of a population as it is distributed spatially.[10] These concepts, which are substantially related to Newton's Law of Gravitation and the contributions of other physicists, are designed to aid in the organization of social physics.

A major concept in this group is potential of population. This concept refers to the influence that people exert on each other at a distance. Stewart has found from the empirical examination of demographic and other social statistics that, in many instances, this influence varies directly with the size of the population and inversely with the distance from it. Potential of population is measured by the formula:

$$V_Q = \frac{P}{r} \dots\dots\dots\dots\dots\dots\dots\dots\dots \text{(1)}$$

1. V_Q is the potential which a population concentration, P, creates at a distant point, Q.
2. r is the distance between Q and P.

Population potential can be illustrated as follows: The distance of New York City from St. Louis is 875 miles. A special population census conducted in New York City in April, 1957 revealed that the city had a total population of 7,785,471. Consequently, the potential at St. Louis produced by the 7,785,471 people of New York is 7,785,471/875, or 8,898 persons per mile.

The total potential at any point is produced by all groups of people. If the distribution of population can be regarded as continuous over a surface, social physics uses the following formula to compute total potential:[11]

---

pp. 42–43 of this study) suggests that he believes that the data of human phenomena should govern the course of scientific investigation. Moreover, in discussing his concept of the development of science, he describes Kepler's development of empirical regularities on the orbital motions of planets as follows: "Kepler made trials, errors, retrials [using Brahe's data]—many of them 'cock-eyed'—before he succeeded in stating the last of his three 'laws' on the orbital motion of the planets." Stewart, "A Basis for Social Physics," p. 114.

[10]Stewart and Warntz, "Physics of Population Distribution," p. 110; John Q. Stewart, "Demographic Gravitation: Evidence and Applications," *Sociometry* (February–May, 1948), p. 32.

[11]The relationship between the social physics concept of population potential and physics can be demonstrated as follows:
Newton's Law of Gravitation may be expressed by the formula:

$$F = \frac{GMm}{d^2}$$

$$V_Q = \int \frac{1}{r} D dA \dots\dots\dots\dots\dots\dots\dots (2)$$

1. V_Q is the aggregate potential at any point Q.
2. D is the density of population over any infinitesimal element of area dA.
3. r is the distance from each said element to the given point Q.

The total potential at St. Louis produced by all the people in the United States can be computed approximately by arbitrarily cutting the United States into a number of districts and measuring the average distance of each district to St. Louis. The population of each district is divided by its distance, and the resultant quotients are summed to give the potential at St. Louis.[12]

A review of the literature of social physics indicates that, thus far, potential of population has been found by social physicists to be the most useful concept. The importance which social physics attaches to potential of population is reflected in the following statement by Stewart and Warntz:

> A measurable factor of great sociological importance exists which can be called "sociological intensity." This is much like its counterpart temperature in the physical world. Not residing or measurable in any one individual in the system, it is nevertheless the result of the combined influence of all, and this influence necessarily varies geographically. In a single macroscopic, integrative index, potential of population, as the leading component in sociological intensity, introduces a powerful unifying concept into the study of human behavior. It can be interpreted as a measure of the interaction of people.[13]

One use to which social physicists put the concept of population potential is in the drawing of a map showing contours of potential.

M is a particle of mass at point A, at a distance d from a second particle of mass m at point a; a force F acts on each mass, attracting them together along the line joining them; G is a universal constant, the gravitational constant.

The gravitational potential V_A which the mass m produces at point A is:

$$V_A = \frac{Gm}{d}$$

The gravitational potential V_a which the mass M produces at point a is:

$$V_a = \frac{GM}{d}$$

See Stewart, "Demographic Gravitation: Evidence and Applications," pp. 32–33.
[12]Stewart, "Potential of Population and Its Relationship to Marketing," pp. 21, 22, and 39.
[13]John Q. Stewart and William Warntz, "Macrogeography and Social Science," *Geographical Review* (April, 1958), pp. 183–184.

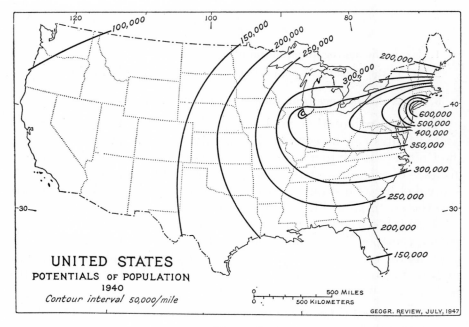

Figure 2

Source: J. Q. Stewart, "Empirical Mathematical Rules Concerning the Distribution
and Equilibrium of Population," *Geographical Review* (July, 1947), p. 476.

In order to draw such a map it is necessary to compute values of
potential for a sufficiently large number of appropriately spaced
"control points." The contours shown on such a map are lines of
equipotential. Examples of equipotential maps are shown in Figures 2
and 3.

Gradient is another basic concept of social physics. It is measured
by the following formula:

$$g = \frac{\partial V}{\partial n} \quad \dots\dots\dots\dots\dots\dots\dots\dots\dots\dots\dots\dots\dots\dots\dots (3)$$

1. g is gradient.
2. ∂V is the change in potential between two contours of equipotential.
3. ∂n is the distance between the relevant contours of equipotential.

Gradient is measured in terms of persons per mile squared.[14] This
is so because potential is population divided by distance and is, therefore, expressed in units of persons per mile. Gradient involves one more

---

[14]In physics the quantity g is the acceleration of any mass produced by the gravitational field. However, in social physics, it is used only as the gradient of potential.
See Stewart, "Demographic Gravitation: Evidence and Applications," pp. 33–34.

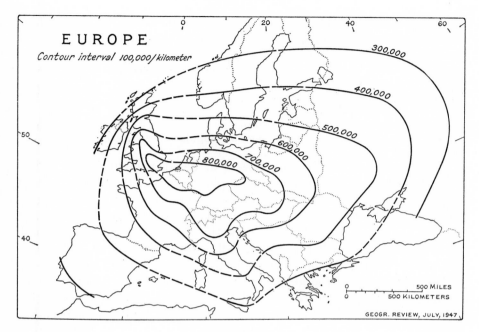

EUROPE
Contour interval 100,000/kilometer

300,000
400,000
500,000
600,000
700,000
800,000

500 MILES
500 KILOMETERS

GEOGR. REVIEW, JULY, 1947

Figure 3

Source: J. Q. Stewart, "Empirical Mathematical Rules Concerning the Distribution and Equilibrium of Population," *Geographical Review* (July, 1947), p. 477.

power of distance in the denominator and, therefore, is in terms of the unit persons per mile squared.

The concept of gradient refers to the change in population potential per mile as one moves closer to, or away from a cluster of population. For example, as one moves from rural areas toward a large city there is a rise in potential because of the concentration of people there; and the gradient becomes steeper as the boundary of the city is approached. Stewart writes that inside the city the population potential and gradient continue to rise — all along the way to the center if the city is roughly circular.

The familiar concept of population density is also used in social physics. This concept originated in physics where the mechanical conception of density refers to the quantity of mass in a unit of volume.[15]

Demographic energy is another basic concept of social physics. This concept refers to the interchange, or human relations, between

[15]Stewart and Warntz, "Macrogeography and Social Science," p. 183.

clusters of people.   Demographic energy acts along the line joining relevant groups of people.   It is measured by the equation:

$$E = \frac{P_1 P_2}{r} \dots\dots\dots\dots\dots\dots\dots\dots\dots\dots \textbf{(4)}$$

1. E is demographic energy.
2. P_1 is one population group.
3. P_2 is another population group.
4. r is the distance between the two population groups.

Demographic energy is expressed in persons squared per mile.[16] In explaining the concept of demographic energy, Stewart writes that when one group of people is placed close to another each is subjected to the other's field, and the result is a strong interaction between the two clusters.   In many instances, he states, the interaction can be measured, e.g., the number of telephone calls interchanged or passenger-automobile traffic.   According to Stewart, the number of calls or cars in a given time will be found, on the average, to be proportional to the product of the two populations divided by the distance separating them.[17]   In this connection it is interesting to note that Stewart regards Reilly's Law of Retail Gravitation as an example of the operation of demographic energy.

Social Physics: Empirical Regularities

It will be recalled that the discovery of empirical regularities is the current principal objective of social physicists.   Just as was the case in physics, the collection of such regularities is a necessary prelude, according to Stewart, to later theoretical understanding.

Stewart defines an empirical regularity as a mathematical statement applicable to a group of observed data.   It is a relationship which has been inductively suggested within a very narrow field of phenomena

---

[16]The concept of demographic energy is based on Newton's equation for the mutual energy of two masses in the gravitational field:

$$E = \frac{GMm}{d}$$

1. G is the gravitational constant.
2. M is a mass at a point.
3. m is a mass at another point.
4. d is the distance between two points.

Mutual energy refers to the force each mass exerts on the other, operating to bring the two masses together.   See Stewart, "Demographic Gravitation: Evidence and Applications," p. 32.

[17]Stewart, "A Basis for Social Physics," p. 119.

where an adequate general pattern of theoretical abstract laws is not
yet available. While an empirical regularity describes the relationship
among relevant social phenomena, it does not explain the relationship.

An empirical regularity frequently cited by Stewart is the rank-size
rule. This rule, $R^n S_R = M$, applies to certain groups of cities. In this
equation M and n are constants for the given group; n is a constant
exponent while M is the population of the largest city. S_R stands for
the number of people who live in the Rth city in the group, and R is the
rank in the group of that city. The rank is a city's order number in a
list that runs consecutively from the largest city in the given group to
the smallest one. According to the 1940 census, various cities in the
United States had the following ranks, R: New York, 1; Chicago, 2;
Philadelphia, 3; . . . ; Utica, 92; . . . ; Sharon, Pennsylvania, 401; etc.

The rank so defined is necessarily a positive integer. When R is 1,
whatever the value of n, S is equal to M. Therefore, the constant M is
equal to the size of the largest city in the group.

Another empirical rule in social physics states that the density of
rural population through geographic space varies as the square of the
population potential. The mathematical form of this statement is:

$$D_R = k V_T^2 \dots\dots\dots\dots\dots\dots\dots\dots\dots(5)$$

1. V_T is the potential of population at any point produced by the total
   population.
2. D_R is the rural density at and near the given point.
3. k is a constant for the isolated human grouping that is being
   considered, e.g., United States or Europe.

The proportionality of the area of a city to its population is another
empirical rule of social physics. This statement is written mathematically as follows:

$$A = \frac{P^{3/4}}{C}$$

1. A is the area of a city.
2. P is the population of that city.
3. C is a constant applicable to a group of cities in a particular country
   during a particular year.

These empirical regularities are general rules in that the stated
relationships have been found to apply intertemporally and interna-
tionally. Social physics also includes empirical rules which are less
general because research to date has shown them to apply over time to

only one country or in one country during a particular year. In empirical rules of the latter type, social physicists present the relevant mathematical statement with a specific figure for the constant involved.

Stewart has found, for example, that there existed in 1940 a relationship between that proportion of the United States population which was classified as urban and the number of cities with a population in excess of 2,500. The mathematical statement of this empirical regularity is:

$$U = 0.009782 \ C$$

1. U is the fraction of the total population that lives in cities with more than 2,500 population.
2. C is the number of cities with populations in excess of 2,500.

Social physics includes other examples of empirical rules which were valid only in the United States and only in 1940. In studying the 1940 census data for the 28-state sequence from Maine to Texas, Stewart found that a variety of sociological phenomena varied with the spatial variation of the potential of population (V). Some of his findings are stated mathematically as follows:

1. Rural nonfarm population density $= 0.000562 \ V^3$.
2. Rural density $= 0.0336 \ V^2$.
3. Farmland values $= 0.050 \ V^2$.
4. Miles of railroad track per square mile $= 0.00413 \ V$.
5. Miles of rural free delivery routes per square mile $= 0.00517 \ V^{3/2}$.
6. Rural nonfarm rents $= 0.556 \ V$.

Social Physics: Methodology

The above discussion of social physics demonstrates the substantial kinship between the physics of natural science and its social counterpart. The physical basis of social physical concepts is clear. This is particularly true of the study of individuals in the mass rather than as individual molecules, which is reflected in the substitution of numbers of people for mass in the relevant equations of physics.

Another major characteristic of social physics revealed by the above discussion is its empirical basis. Concepts are measurable in terms of observable phenomena, and the relationship existing among social phenomena are sought through study of relevant data. Population and distance are major independent variables in the scheme of social physics.

Table III

EVIDENCE FOR THE RELATION OF THE AREA TO THE
POPULATION OF UNITED STATES CITIES, 1940

Rank of City	Log C	Rank of City	Log C	Rank of City	Log C
1	2.67	31–35	2.44	151–165	2.61
2	2.59	36–40	2.48	166–180	2.60
3	2.62	41–45	2.41	181–195	2.55
4	2.47	46–50	2.45	196–210	2.65
5	1.98	51–55	2.54	211–225	2.54
6	2.60	56–60	2.41	226–240	2.56
7	2.55	61–65	2.58	241–255	2.56
8	2.64	66–70	2.54	256–270	2.61
9	2.76	71–75	2.59	271–285	2.48
10	2.65	76–80	2.51	286–300	2.57
11	2.58	81–85	2.63	301–315	2.52
12	2.70	86–90	2.64	316–330	2.53
13	2.70	91–95	2.48	331–345	2.63
14	2.73	96–100	2.62	346–360	2.48
15	1.98	101–105	2.69	361–375	2.52
16–20	2.49	106–120	2.58	376–390	2.51
21–25	2.37	121–135	2.55	391–405	2.46
26–30	2.52	136–150	2.68	406–412	2.55

Log C is the logarithm to the base 10 of C, where $C = \dfrac{P^{3/4}}{A}$, P being the population of any city and A the land area in square miles within its political boundaries (Census of 1940). The rank in the first column is the order of their population size, New York being rank 1, Chicago 2, etc. The largest 15 cities are listed individually. After that only medians are listed — of groups of 5 cities each to rank 105, then of groups of 15 for the smaller cities. Where medians are tabulated, P is the median population of the group and A the median land area.

Source: John Q. Stewart and William Warntz, "Physics of Population Distribution," *Journal of Regional Science* (Summer, 1958), p. 100.

The empirical method of social physics is illustrated by the method used to discover the empirical rule[18] $A = \dfrac{P^{3/4}}{C}$.

Table III presents the original statistics which suggested this rule. The equation relating area and population was found by a linear least squares solution of the logarithmic values of the population data contained in this table. This method of arriving at an empirical rule is

---

[18]It will be recalled from page 43 that A is the area of a city, P is its population, and C is a constant applicable to a group of cities in a particular country during a particular year.

typical of the method used by Stewart and his associate social physicists.[19]

Social physicists regard the empirical rule $A = \frac{P^{3/4}}{C}$ as having inter-
temporal and international validity, since it is based on data pertaining
to United States cities extending back at least to 1890 and more recent
data for cities in England and Wales.[20]

Social physics acceptance of the rank-size rule as a general empirical
rule is based on a study of United States cities having a population
greater than 2,500 in the 16 censuses taken during the period 1790–
1940. For each of these censuses, Stewart writes, the rank-size rule
holds approximately, and always with n equal to 1, or nearly 1.[21]
Stewart does not present the data on the basis of which he makes this
statement, nor does he give any measure which reveals how closely the
rank-size rule fits the city population data provided by each census.
He does state that he did not use the least squares technique of analysis
because "this is time-consuming, and for purposes of the present survey
adequate solutions have been obtained by trial and error or by graph-
ing."[22]

Stewart presents the data in Table IV as constituting "observa-
tional confirmation of the applicability of the rank-size rule"[23] for each
of the censuses during the period 1790–1940.

The data in Table IV do not contravene the rank-size rule, but they
are not sufficient to validate it. This is so because the data only show
that the product of the population of the smallest city and its rank
roughly equals the size of the largest city. While this is in accordance
with the rank-size rule, the data do not deal with the applicability of
the rule to the other cities in the group during any one census year.
That is, the data in Table IV are inadequate to support Stewart's
assertion that:

> . . . it is a fact that when all the cities in the United States larger
> than 2500 (or than some lower limit greater than 2500) are examined

---

[19]See, for example, John Q. Stewart, "Empirical Mathematical Rules Concerning
the Distribution and Equilibrium of Population," *Geographical Review* (July, 1947),
pp. 468–483; and Stewart, "Demographic Gravitation: Evidence and Application,"
pp. 40–47.

[20]Stewart and Warntz, "Physics of Population Distribution," pp. 100–104.

[21]Stewart, "Empirical Mathematical Rules Concerning the Distribution and
Equilibrium of Population," p. 463.

[22]*Ibid.*, p. 464.

[23]*Ibid.*, p. 465.

Table IV

DATA PRESENTED BY STEWART AS
SUBSTANTIATION OF APPLICABILITY OF RANK-SIZE RULE

Census	C^a	Log M Observed Values[b]	Log M_e Computed Values[c]
1790	24	4.69	4.78
1800	33	4.90	4.92
1810	46	5.08	5.06
1820	61	5.18	5.18
1830	90	5.38	5.35
1840	131	5.59	5.52
1850	236	5.85	5.77
1860	392	6.07	5.99
1870	663	6.17	6.22
1880	939	6.28	6.37
1890	1,348	6.40	6.53
1900	1,737	6.54	6.64
1910	2,262	6.58	6.75
1920	2,732	6.75	6.84
1930	3,165	6.84	6.90
1940	3,464	6.87	6.94

a. C is the number of cities with a population exceeding 2,500.
b. M is the actual population of the largest city revealed by each census.
c. M_c is the computed value of M obtained by taking the product of 2,500 and the value of C.

Source: John Q. Stewart, "Empirical Mathematical Rules Concerning the Distribution and Equilibrium of Population," *Geographical Review* (July, 1947), p. 466.

in any one of the 16 censuses 1790–1940, equation 1 (the rank-size rule) holds approximately, and always with n equal to 1, or nearly 1.[24]

If Stewart had made a least-squares analysis of the city data for each census year, he could have computed coefficients of determination which would have permitted a judgment as to how close the rank-size rule fit these data. He could have computed S_R, using the rank-size rule, and then calculated coefficients of determination which would have revealed the extent to which the variation in the actual city sizes could be "explained" by reference to S_R.

Pitirim A. Sorokin, a critic of social physics, has also studied the

[24]*Ibid.*, p. 463.

validity of the rank-size rule as applied to city sizes and has concluded that no such rule exists. He writes that an examination of the 1940 census data reveals that:

> ... the rank-size rule is a fairly loose rule; since the product of the size and the rank of the cities varies from 5,794,000 to 10,300,000 or within a ratio of 5 to 9, it is difficult to claim such a product constant. Such a constancy seems to be notably inconstant. It becomes much more variant if we take the population of the cities in 1840. Then the product of the rank and the size of only the 17 biggest cities fluctuate from 391,114 (New York) to 67,050 (Chicago) — that is, our constant for New York is six times larger than that for Chicago. In this case there is hardly any possibility of talking even about a loose constant. The rank-size rule simply doesn't exist for 1840. It is even less in evidence if we take the census data for 1790, 1800, and other years of the census. If the rule is tested on the cities of other countries, there is practically nothing left of the rank-size rule.[25]

Social physics' development of empirical rules which show that a wide variety of social phenomena vary with spatial variation in potentials of population is illustrated by the following study by Stewart, which is based on the data in Table V. These data show that the numbers of students at Phillips Exeter from the several states vary directly with the potential of population of the states of origin at Exeter, New Hampshire.

Column (2) of Table V is the potential of population of each state at Exeter, New Hampshire. Column (4) contains estimates obtained by using the following empirical rule:

1. Number of students from a state $= .25V_Q$.
2. V_Q is the population potential of a state at Exeter, New Hampshire.

The data in column (4) of Table V that are enclosed in parentheses refer to nine southern and eleven western states. Stewart and Warntz enclose them in parentheses to indicate that for the southern states the actual numbers would run consistently low, and for the western states high, if weighting factors of eight-tenths and two, respectively, had not been applied to the "expected numbers." On the basis of various studies such as these, Stewart and Warntz have concluded that, as regards potential of population, each person in the nine southern states

---

[25]Pitirim A. Sorokin, *Fads and Foibles in Modern Sociology and Related Sciences,* (Chicago: Henry Regnery Company, 1956), p. 119.

Table V
GEOGRAPHICAL DISTRIBUTION OF
PHILLIPS EXETER STUDENTS

State (1)	Potential (2)	Number of Students Actual (3)	"Expected" (4)
New York	531	162	133
Massachusetts	470	134	118
Pennsylvania	278	38	70
Connecticut	160	48	40
New Jersey	145	42	36
Maine	135	9	34
Ohio	118	20	30
New Hampshire	109	42	27
Illinois	103	21	26
Michigan	93	9	23
Rhode Island	74	2	19
Virginia	53	9	(10)
North Carolina	53	7	(10)
Indiana	48	5	12
Maryland	48	4	12
Texas	45	15	11
Vermont	41	9	10
California	38	15	(19)
Missouri	38	4	10
Wisconsin	36	7	9
Kentucky	35	7	9
Tennessee	32	6	(6)
Georgia	31	3	(6)
West Virginia	29	7	7
Minnesota	27	3	7
Alabama	25	9	(5)
Iowa	23	10	6
South Carolina	23	3	(4)
Florida	20	9	5
District of Columbia	18	5	5
Louisiana	18	1	(4)
Mississippi	16	4	(3)
Oklahoma	16	2	(4)
Arkansas	15	4	(3)
Kansas	14	0	3
Nebraska	10	2	3
Washington	10	7	5
Delaware	8	4	2
Colorado	7	1	3
Oregon	7	2	(3)
North Dakota	4	0	1
South Dakota	4	0	1
Utah	4	2	(2)
Arizona	3	2	(2)
Idaho	3	1	(1)
Montana	3	0	(1)
New Mexico	3	2	(2)
Wyoming	2	4	(2)
Nevada	0.6	1	(1)

Source: John Q. Stewart and William Warntz, "Macrogeography and Social Science,"
   Geographical Review (April, 1958), p. 169.

should be given a "molecular weight" of 0.8; whereas, each person in the eleven states should be given a "molecular weight" of 2.0.[26]

If the data in column (3) are regarded as the dependent variable, the data in column (4) as the independent variable, and a correlation analysis is performed, a coefficient of determination equal to .88 is obtained. This means that 88 per cent of the variation in the actual number of students attending Phillips Exeter is "explained" by reference to the adjusted estimate obtained through use of the empirical rule:

$$\text{Number of students from a state}[27] = .25V_Q.$$

If these calculations had yielded a coefficient of determination of 1.0, it would have meant that the actual number of students attending Phillips Exeter from each state could be precisely predicted by use of this empirical rule, with appropriate adjustment of the results by the relevant molecular weights.

In Table V the average absolute deviation of the expected values from the actual data is 5.5 students, while the average relative deviation is 8.8 per cent. If the data in this table are arranged in class intervals, the largest relative error is found in the 11–30 range, and the largest absolute deviation occurs in the 31 and above interval.

Similar studies were made by Stewart for other schools, e.g., Harvard, Yale, Princeton, with respect to the flow of bank checks into New York from Federal Reserve branch districts and with respect to the presence at a given point of passenger automobiles originating in various states. These studies provide additional evidence leading social physicists to conclude that a wide variety of social phenomena vary with spatial variation in potentials of population.

United States census data for each of the censuses conducted from 1790–1940 provide the evidence for an empirical rule relating the number of United States cities to the fraction of the population that lives in cities.

---

[26]Stewart and Warntz, "Macrogeography and Social Science," p. 169. According to Stewart, "when the potentials produced by people of different sorts are computed, it is necessary for comparability of results to make the formula (population divided by distance) include a weighting factor or 'molecular weight' by which each population is multiplied. Even within the United States, the evidence requires a range of more than 2 to 1 in the molecular weight in different parts of the country. Although numerical data are not available it is certain that the relative influence at a distance produced by primitive savages is very much less than that of people in an advanced state of material civilization." See Stewart, "A Basis for Social Physics," p. 121.

[27]After this computation is made, the result, when appropriate, is adjusted for "molecular weight."

Social physicists do not claim that their empirical regularities permit exact predictions. In one study Stewart writes:

> . . . we must guard against giving the impression that any one of the empirical rules presented is at all exact and, on the other, against suggesting that the approximations are so rough as to be without profound interest and meaning.[28]

Elsewhere Stewart and Warntz conclude that if any empirical rule has a coefficient of correlation exceeding 0.70 this is "an indication that the results are highly significant."[29]

Thus far in the development of social physics Stewart and his associate social physicists have concentrated their efforts on the collection of empirical regularities. They have not made many attempts to explain the regularities they have found or their significance.

Here and there in the literature of social physics, however, comments are found relating to one or another of the social physical empirical rules. In one study Stewart says that the rank-size rule is an important empirical relation with the presumption that it is the result of major underlying demographic tendencies. Elsewhere, he states that the tendency of rural density to be proportional to the square of the population potential indicates that the United States possesses "demographic unity of a certain type."[30] In another study he states that the empirical rule relating the number of United States cities and the urban fraction points to an equilibrium between the rural and urban population.

Despite comments such as these, the following statement appears to be still applicable not only to the rank-size rule but also to other empirical regularities of social physics:

> Readers whose training has been verbal rather than mathematical may be impatient to be told at once what the underlying reasons are for the rank-size rule and what applications it has to immediately practical problems. These are reasonable inquiries, but their answers can only come in due course, and such readers will be blind to the

---

[28]Stewart, "Empirical Mathematical Rules Concerning the Distribution and Equilibrium of Population," p. 462.

[29]Stewart and Warntz, "Macrogeography and Social Science," p. 172. In a letter to the author dated February 17, 1963 Stewart wrote: "Warntz and I have never set up a correlation coefficient of 0.7 as enough for establishing a rule. When the same rule occurs again and again with widely different data you have a situation not adequately covered by mere correlations. And when an initial regularity leads to new ones as with the subject of potential of population, again you are beyond mere mathematical statistics."

[30]Stewart, "Potential of Population and Its Relation to Marketing," p. 23.

lessons of physical science if they lose patience and interest when it is confessed that full answers cannot yet be provided.[31]

Social Physics : Some Evaluatory Comments

Social physicists have as their ultimate objective the formulation of theories and laws of human behavior. However, these are ultimate objectives which, Stewart implies, cannot be attained until after social physics makes progress during its current stage which emphasizes the discovery of mathematical empirical regularities.[32]

The extent to which social physicists, such as Stewart and Warntz, have collected empirical regularities has been indicated in preceding pages.[33] Its induction together with deduction methodology is, of course, a commonly used tool of scientific investigation. Social physicists apparently use a coefficient of correlation of 0.7 as a lower limit for deciding whether a particular empirical relationship is potentially useful. The unique aspect of the social physics approach lies in its attempt to study human behavior in the way that the physical scientist has studied matter.

On the basis of the progress which social physics has made to date, it does not appear feasible to make a firm evaluation of the usefulness of this approach other than to say that social physics is apparently some distance from attaining its objective. Stewart's belief in the attainability of the goals of social physics rests on his faith in the existence of natural law in human behavior. In a letter to this writer he stated:

> When the American Constitution was framed in Philadelphia in 1787, the leaders of the convention believed in the existence of natural laws relating to human behavior — just as they were deeply impressed by the then still rather novel statement by Newton and others of natural laws in celestial mechanics and physical science.

---

[31]Stewart, "Empirical Mathematical Rules Concerning the Distribution and Equilibrium of Population," p. 463.

[32]Stewart does not explicity state what he views to be the relationship between empirical regularity, theory, and law. However, study of Stewart's writings suggest the following: An empirical regularity is valid with respect to a segment of some phenomenon while a law has general validity with respect to this phenomenon—e.g., empirical regularity: Kepler's statements describing the orbital motion of planets; law: Newton's laws of motion. A theory is an explanation, the underlying rationale, of an empirical regularity or law. Thus, the development of theories and laws in social physics follow and depend on the prior discovery of empirical regularities. Stewart, for example, accepts the rank-size rule as being observable in many types of social statistics in addition to city populations. He would be willing to accept this rule as a law of social physics if its underlying rationale could be determined. See Stewart, "A Basis for Social Physics," pp. 115–16.

[33]Others who have contributed to social physics, according to Stewart, are: Lester F. Ward, Simon Newcomb, Emile Durkheim, P. W. Bridgman, Stuart C. Dodd, and George K. Zipf.

This set of beliefs has gradually been lost in political and other social sciences.

But not for valid reasons. Social Physics is not radical but conservative, in that it still attempts to apply that original faith in scientific method.[34]

The failure of social physicists to discover any such natural laws to date, of course, does not prove that they do not exist or that they cannot be ascertained, anymore than man's failure to put a space satellite in orbit prior to 1957 proved that this feat could not be accomplished.

Recent social physics literature reflects the struggling efforts that are being made either to explain the empirical relationships that have been found to date or to assess their significance within some overall scheme. The paucity of such analyses seems to indicate that the collection of empirical regularities has not yet made sufficient progress to enable social physicists to attain considerable theoretical understanding of the social phenomena which they are studying.

In his evaluation of social physics, Sorokin, as noted above, has been highly critical of this approach. Among the observations that Sorokin makes is the following:

Wherever and whenever the psychological problems lend themselves to real measurements, to real homological treatment, it is advisable to use such measurements and homologies; but they in no way eliminate direct study and measurements of these phenomena by means of a conceptual framework and the methods built by these sciences in accordance with the nature of the phenomena studied. A mere transformation of the terms, concepts and methods of physical sciences into the social and psychological disciplines, and a mere analogical reasoning, has not yielded, and cannot yield, any fruitful results in cognition of the psychosocial universe of man and of the total man himself.[35]

This critical position is not shared by George A. Lundberg who appears to be of the opinion that social physics has made worthwhile contributions to science. In reviewing George K. Zipf's book, *Human Behavior and Least Effort*,[36] in which Zipf presents the rank-size rule among other empirical regularities, Lundberg makes the following comment:

---

[34]Letter from John Q. Stewart, April 6, 1959.

[35]Sorokin, *Fads and Foibles in Modern Sociology*, pp. 187–195.

[36]G. K. Zipf, *Human Behavior and Least Effort* (Cambridge: Addison-Wesley Press, 1949).

When all the complaints and criticisms have been made, however, it will not be possible to deny, I think, that Dr. Zipf has produced one of the most stimulating books of our time. There are presented here a remarkable number and variety of observations which have unmistakable implications as empirical natural laws, regardless of the theoretical interpretations that anyone wishes to propose.

In the meantime, there is presented in this book something that has hitherto been sadly lacking in the social sciences and especially in ecology, namely a comprehensive rational theory and a wealth of supporting empirical data which, whatever may be the limitations of both at this stage of development, nevertheless represents a bold, imaginative, and brilliant approach toward a natural science of human behavior.[37]

While social physics is still essentially in the stage of the collection of empirical regularities, this field is, nevertheless, of interest and of potential usefulness to students of marketing. Among the independent variables on which social physics focuses are clusters of people and distances between population concentrations. These variables have been observed to determine the marketing behavior of people and the operation of marketing agencies. For this reason, mathematical generalizations based on these variables would be a welcome addition to marketing science. The related social physical concepts of population potential and demographic energy are consistent with the results found by Reilly in his study of retail trade areas and suggest that it may be fruitful to probe further into the effect on marketing of distance and clusters of people.

---

[37]George Lundberg, "Review of Human Behavior and Least Effort," *Annals of the American Academy of Political and Social Science* (July, 1949), pp. 186–187.

Chapter 4

THEORY OF GAMES OF STRATEGY

Game theory as a mathematical discipline was initiated by John von Neumann in 1928[1] and developed further by him in 1940–41. The mathematical principles were first applied to economics in 1944 when von Neumann collaborated with Oskar Morgenstern to publish *Theory of Games and Economic Behavior.*[2]

Although this volume focused attention on the utility of game theory with respect to problems of economic theory, scholars and analysts in a number of other fields, e.g., management science, sociology, and military science, have since been stimulated to investigate the applicability of the theory to problems in their respective areas of interest. The result has been a large literature that applies the theory to areas beyond those developed by von Neumann and Morgenstern.[3]

Von Neumann-Morgenstern Approach to Theory

A basic idea of game theory is that economic markets, parlor games, and military battles are all instances of social situations in which the participants pursue partly conflicting and partly mutual interests. The fate of each participant, e.g., a salesman's commission or a wholesaler's profits, depends in part on his own actions and in part on the actions of the other participants. Such situations, in which the outcome

---

[1]John von Neumann, "Zur Theorie der Gesellschaftspiele," *Mathematische Annalen,* Vol. 100 (1928), pp. 295–320.

[2]John von Neumann and Oskar Morgenstern, *Theory of Games and Economic Behavior* (Princeton: Princeton University Press). This volume has been published in three editions—1944, 1947, and 1953. Footnote references to the book in this chapter apply to the third edition.

[3]An interestingly written and illuminating book on game theory is that by J. D. Williams, *The Compleat Strategyst* (New York: McGraw Hill Book Company, Inc., 1954). For bibliographies on game theory see: Robert D. Luce and Howard Raiffa, *Games and Decisions* (New York: John Wiley & Sons, Inc., 1957), pp. 485–499; J. C. C. McKinsey, *Introduction to the Theory of Games* (New York: McGraw-Hill Book Company, Inc., 1952), pp. 361–367; and David H. Blackwell and M. A. Girschick, *Theory of Games and Statistical Decisions* (New York: John Wiley & Sons, Inc., 1954), pp. 337–345.

is controlled jointly by a number of participants, is similar in many respects to games involving the use of strategy.

Game theory analyzes behavior through the use of games as models of social situations. According to von Neumann and Morgenstern, these models are "theoretical constructs with a precise, exhaustive and not too complicated definition; and they must be similar to reality in those respects which are essential in the investigation at hand."[4] Models having these characteristics are said to be: (1) amenable to mathematical analysis yielding numerical results and (2) operationally significant.[5]

In analyzing their models of conflict situations, game theorists make extensive use of modern mathematical methods. These theorists reject the position of those who argue that mathematics is not useful in the social sciences because of the human element, the psychological factor, and the difficulty of measuring important variables. Von Neumann and Morgenstern believe that there exists no fundamental reason why mathematics should not be used in social science. They do believe, however, that the effective scientific study of social phenomena may require the discovery of new mathematical methods in addition to those used in game theory.

Von Neumann and Morgenstern hold the view that a theory should be developed by stages. In the early phases of the development of a theory, simple situations should be studied, e.g., the economic behavior of the individual and the simplest form of exchange. The first applications of a theory are to elementary problems where the results have never been in doubt and no theory is actually required. In the next phase the theory is applied to more complicated situations and produces conclusions that are to some extent beyond the obvious and the familiar. The final phase in the development of a theory is reached when it is capable of prediction regardless of the complexity of the relevant situation to which it is applied.

Von Neumann and Morgenstern write that all mathematical sciences have gone through such successive phases of evolution. In their opinion a newly developed theory cannot be finally accepted as a scientific theory unless it includes a mathematical proof of its conclusion. The final form of a theory must, they assert, be mathematically rigorous and conceptually general.

---

[4]Von Neumann and Morgenstern, *op. cit.* p. 32.
[5]*Ibid.* Operationally significant, in this context, means that these numerical results are useful in making choice decisions in actual social situations.

Many economists are criticized by von Neumann and Morgenstern for being, in their opinion, unwilling to accept the "fact" that theory must progress from the simple to the complicated. They write:

> These economists frequently point to much larger, more "burning" questions, and brush everything aside which prevents them from making statements about these. The experience of more advanced sciences, for example, physics, indicates that this impatience merely delays progress, including that of the treatment of the "burning" questions.[6]

Von Neumann and Morgenstern assert that there is no reason to assume the existence of shortcuts in the development of theory and science.[7]

Game Theory: Analytical Procedure

Game theory classifies game models in several ways. One classification is based on the number of players participating in the game. A "player" is a specific interest or coalition of interests in a conflict situation. It may be one person, an enterprise, or a coalition of individuals or enterprises. In a situation where each of three salesmen is attempting to get a particular order, for example, the game may be said to have three players. Correspondingly, where two integrated marketing channels compete with each other for the patronage of a particular customer or a particular group of customers, the game is said to involve two players.

Another classification divides games into zero-sum and nonzero-sum games. In a zero-sum game what one player wins, others lose. A nonzero-sum game can be either a constant-sum or a variable-sum game. In the constant-sum game the aggregate amount that the players can win is of a specific magnitude; in the variable-sum game, this magnitude varies within some specified range.

Game theory holds that games involving two players are substantially different from games involving a larger number. It also holds that the analytical problems posed by variable-sum games are more complex than those presented by zero-sum and constant-sum games. When the number of players is larger than two, the major new factor is that the identities of the persons may change in the course of the game

---

[6]*Ibid.* p. 7.

[7]*Ibid.* Von Neumann and Morgenstern do not provide the evidence necessary to support the statements included in this paragraph. For example, it is not self-evident that shortcuts in the development of theory and science do not exist.

as temporary coalitions are formed and broken, or certain players may form what is in effect a permanent coalition in some area of action where they conceive it to be beneficial. In variable-sum games coalitions will also be formed if the coalition can earn more than the total the individuals can earn by playing independently. This gives rise to the problems of how the excess should be divided and what system of sidepayments should be made among the players to ensure that the coalition will prosper and that the members will remain loyal.

In its present phase of development, game theory is largely a static theory; that is, it deals with equilibria, and the essential characteristic of an equilibrium is that it has no tendency to change.[8] In analyzing various types of games, game theory seeks to specify an equilibrium solution for any conflict situation. Such a solution sets forth the courses of action rational players would take in a conflict situation and the resultant gains or losses which would accrue to the players. A statement of how the proceeds of a game will be divided among the players is termed an imputation. Game theory's concept of rationality holds that the intelligent player tries to gain as much from the game as he can safely gain in the face of skillful adversaries who are pursuing opposing goals.[9]

Game Theory: Analytical Illustrations

It will be recalled that a game may be any conflict situation, such as one involving the firms in an industry which are vying with each other in an attempt to increase their sales. It will also be recalled that an important characteristic of this type of situation is that the extent to which the marketing efforts of each enterprise are successful depends not only on its own skill and resources but also on the marketing behavior of competing enterprises. In this type of situation, game theory analyzes the alternatives available to the players and seeks to arrive at an equilibrium solution.

In game theory an equilibrium solution is that method of playing a game which maximizes the gain accruing to any player or minimizes the

---

[8]Von Neumann and Morgenstern state that a dynamic theory would be more preferable because it would be more complete. However, they write that "it is futile to try to build one as long as the static side is not thoroughly understood." See von Neumann and Morgenstern, *op. cit.*, p. 44.

[9]Von Neumann and Morgenstern write: "Our approach should be compared with the widely held view that a social theory is possible only on the basis of some preconceived principles of social purpose. These principles would include quantitative statements concerning both the aims to be achieved *in toto* and the apportionment between individuals. Once they are accepted, a simple maximum problem results." See von Neumann and Morgenstern, *op. cit.*, p. 42.

loss suffered by any player. That is, it sets down the specific alternatives which rational players would follow and reveals the payoffs obtained by each player.

In order to illustrate game theory analysis it is necessary, at this point, to introduce the concepts of strategy, payoff, and game matrix. A strategy is an overall plan that specifies what a player will do in every foreseeable contingency. A payoff is what a player gains or loses when he makes a move using one of his strategies and other players make moves using one of their respective strategies. A game matrix is an array of boxes each containing a payoff number.

These terms can be illustrated by the example shown in Figure 4.

XYZ Yeast Company

		(1) $ 50,000	(2) $100,000	(3) $200,000
	Strategies			
	(1) $ 50,000	$500,000	$400,000	$300,000
	(2) $100,000	$600,000	$500,000	$400,000
	(3) $200,000	$700,000	$600,000	$500,000

ABC Yeast Company (left vertical label)

Figure 4

SADDLE POINT ILLUSTRATION

In this illustration it is assumed that the yeast industry consists of only two companies or players — the XYZ Yeast Company and the ABC Yeast Company. In this conflict situation XYZ, because it fears possible antitrust prosecution, is seeking not to increase its sales but to maintain them at the current level. ABC, however, is aggressively attempting to cut into XYZ's sales.

During the period under discussion it is assumed that each company has only three marketing strategies available to it involving an increase in total expenditures for advertising and personal selling of $50,000, $100,000, and $200,000. Each of the numbers in Figure 4 represents a payoff, or a potential increase in ABC's sales and a concomitant diminution in XYZ's sales. The array of these payoffs is the game matrix. Figure 4 illustrates a zero-sum game because any increase in ABC's sales is accompanied by an equivalent decrease in XYZ's sales; and if one side wins, the other side loses.

An equilibrium solution to this zero-sum game, assuming rational behavior on the part of the decision makers in ABC and XYZ, is obtained by game theory in the following manner. Game theory states that it would be rational for ABC to select strategy (3),[10] i.e., spend $200,000 on advertising and personal selling because this choice would result in ABC's increasing its sales by at least $500,000 regardless of the strategy choice made by XYZ. Since the minimum payoff associated with ABC's strategy (3) is greater than those associated with either strategies (1) or (2), ABC's selection of strategy (3) means that it is maximizing its minimum potential payoff. The latter is referred to as the "maximin."

If XYZ plays the game rationally, it would choose its strategy (3) and also spend $200,000 on advertising and personal selling. This choice is considered rational in game theory because it would minimize the maximum sales gain that ABC could achieve. That is, regardless of which strategy ABC chooses, it could increase its sales by no more than $500,000. A defensive strategy choice which has these characteristics is known as the "minimax."

If both ABC and XYZ made rational decisions in this assumed conflict situation, the equilibrium solution of the game would specify that each company would spend $200,000 on advertising and personal selling, and ABC would increase its sales by $500,000. If ABC behaved rationally but XYZ did not, ABC would increase its sales by more than $500,000.

When the rational strategies of two players intersect at a payoff (as they do in this illustration), the game is said to have a "saddle-point" which is equal to that payoff. In this case the saddle-point is $500,000.[11] The presence of a saddle-point facilitates the determination of equilibrium game solutions. However, saddle-points do not occur frequently in game matrices.[12]

In games that have a saddle-point, it is not necessary for a player to keep his strategy choice secret. Under the conditions assumed in the above illustration, XYZ is unable to prevent ABC from increasing its sales by $500,000 even if ABC announces beforehand that it is going to use strategy (3).

---

[10]See Figure 4.

[11]Game theory uses the term "saddle-point" because the concept is analogous to the shape of a saddle. A saddle has a point which, simultaneously, is the crest of a hill (portion of saddle which fits over horse) and the low point of a valley (portion in which rider sits).

[12]Williams, *The Compleat Strategyst*, p. 27.

Since most games do not have a saddle-point,[13] game theory provides another method for ascertaining the rational strategies of the players. Let us refer to the yeast industry again. In the conflict situation that we postulate, ABC is again attempting to increase its sales at XYZ's expense. The strategies available to each company involve advertising in newspapers or on radio.

Figure 5 shows the amounts by which the ABC Yeast Company can increase its sales given the strategies assumed in this game. This being a zero-sum game, any gain by ABC is the exact amount lost by XYZ.

XYZ Yeast Company

Strategies	(1) Radio	(2) Newspapers
(1) Radio	$400,000	$800,000
(2) Newspapers	$700,000	$500,000

(Rows labeled under "ABC Yeast Company")

Figure 5

MIXED STRATEGY ILLUSTRATION

As is shown in Figure 5, ABC's maximin is $500,000 and XYZ's minimax is $700,000. That is, (1) ABC is assured of a sales increase of $500,000 if it uses newspapers, regardless of XYZ's strategy choice, and (2) if XYZ makes a rational decision, i.e., if it uses radio, ABC cannot increase its sales by more than $700,000 no matter which strategy choice it makes.

In this type of game situation, game theory seeks an equilibrium solution such that ABC increases its sales by an amount greater than $500,000 but less than $700,000. ABC could accomplish this by using a mixed strategy, i.e., sometimes using strategy (1) and sometimes using strategy (2) in a combination determined by preassigned probabilities.[14] The sequence in which the two strategies would be used should be determined by some chance device such as rolling a die.

---

[13]This statement is based on the calculation of probabilities by game theorists. For example, Williams states that in a two-person game in which each player has four strategies (a 4 x 4 game), there is approximately one chance in ten that a matrix of random numbers will have a saddle-point.

[14]A single strategy such as strategy (1) or strategy (2) is known as a "pure strategy." A combination of pure strategies is termed a "mixed strategy."

Game theory advises this procedure in order to prevent XYZ from learning of ABC's strategy choice beforehand and responding with the more effective of the two strategies available to it.

For the simple case illustrated by Figure 5, the probability combination in which ABC should mix its two available pure strategies can be determined by subtracting each figure in column (2) from the figure in the same row of column (1). This procedure yields -4 and 2. According to the mathematics of game theory, this result means that ABC should use a mixed strategy consisting of two plays of strategy (1) to four plays of strategy (2). If ABC used this mixed strategy against XYZ's strategy (1), ABC would increase its sales by $600,000. This result is computed as follows:

$$\frac{2 \times \$400,000 + 4 \times \$700,000}{2 + 4} = \$600,000$$

If ABC used this mixed strategy against XYZ's strategy (2), the attained sales increase would also be $600,000, computed as follows:

$$\frac{2 \times \$800,000 + 4 \times \$500,000}{2 + 4} = \frac{\$3,600,000}{6} = \$600,000$$

Von Neumann and Morgenstern have demonstrated mathematically that in any two-person, zero-sum game without a saddle point, there exists a pair of mixed strategies that constitute an equilibrium solution. If one player adopts his element of the pair, the other participant can do no better than to adopt his element. This is so because these mixed strategies guarantee to each player the most desirable expected payoff that he can obtain against skillful play by his opposition.

Up to this point the exposition of game theory has focused on two-person games. Game theory also analyzes game models having more than two players. In this type of game a new factor is introduced, i.e., the advantage players obtain if they combine against others. The theory treats this type of situation as if coalitions oppose each other in the manner of individual players in a two-person game. However, in the two-person, zero-sum game the theory is able to designate a single best course of action for the players, but games having more than two players are not amenable to such a unique solution. A solution in the latter type of game consists of a set of courses of action and consequent imputations none of which is, *a priori*, superior to the others.

A three-person, zero-sum game can be illustrated by an example involving three bakers of packaged white bread who are competing with each other for larger sales. In this type of situation game theory states that it would be rational for any two of these bakers to combine against another if, by doing so, each could increase his sales by an amount greater than he could by acting alone.[15] In this event a coalition would then oppose the remaining baker in the manner of a two-person, zero-sum game.

Figure 6 presents a matrix showing the sales gains or losses which would accrue to each baker depending on which coalition was formed.

Coalitions \ Bakers	M	I	X
M, I	$20,000	$20,000	−$40,000
M, X	$20,000	−$40,000	$20,000
I, X	−$40,000	$20,000	$20,000

Figure 6

THREE PERSON, ZERO-SUM GAME ILLUSTRATION

The important characteristic of this game is that none of the three imputations shown in Figure 6 is superior to the others. That is, MI, for example, is not an equilibrium solution because this imputation results in a loss for X. X, acting rationally, would therefore seek to combine with M in order to increase his sales by $20,000. But MX is not an equilibrium solution because it involves a loss for I. I, acting rationally, would therefore seek to combine with either M or X, and so on.

In the actual playing of this game, one of the three coalitions and imputations will materialize. Game theory, however, is unable to predict which of these alternative outcomes will take place because none is superior to the others. For this reason the theory regards the three coalitions and imputations shown in Figure 6 as the solution to the game.

Von Neumann's and Morgenstern's general concept of a solution to a game involving more than two players holds that a solution consists of a "stable set" of many different ways of dividing up the

---

[15] A coalition of two companies marketing white bread might be thought of as an arrangement in which both adopt similar rather than opposing marketing policies.

proceeds obtained by joint action. A "stable set" is one consisting of a group of alternative outcomes which stalemate each other. A number of students of game theory have expressed dissatisfaction with this concept of a solution. They are not sure that knowing such a solution would enable an individual to play the game more profitably, especially if the other players did not similarly know the solution.

Game theory, as it has been developed by von Neumann and Morgenstern, primarily analyzes zero-sum games with a small number of players. The fact that their general and systematic theory pertains only to games with 4 players or less stems from the fact that conceptual difficulties arise in obtaining solutions for games having even a small number of participants. These difficulties increase rapidly as the number of players increases. It is known, for example, that all three-person games and all four-person games have solutions, but it has never been shown that all five-person games have solutions.[16]

Von Neumann extends his zero-sum game theory to the solution of nonzero-sum, i.e., variable-sum, games by introducing a fictitious player into the game. The winnings of this player are, by definition, equal to the negative sum of the gains of all the actual players. In this way a variable-sum, n-person game is converted to a zero-sum, $(n + 1)$-person game. Not all of the solutions of the converted game, however, may be taken as solutions of the original game. Only those which meet the condition that the fictitious player cannot exert even an indirect influence on the course of the game solve the original game.

Since the initial publication of *Theory of Games of Economic Behavior* in 1944, a number of other game theorists have built upon the work started by the late von Neumann. One of these theorists, J. F. Nash, has proposed a solution of games involving more than two persons which is different from that of von Neumann and Morgenstern. Whereas the latter arrive at solutions by postulating the formation of coalitions, Nash has tried to construct a theory of noncooperative games for situations in which coalitions are not possible or where they are prohibited by such measures as antitrust legislation. Other game theorists, realizing that many real-life situations do not necessarily involve losses for some players and winnings for others but result in either gains or losses to all players, are trying to find equilibrium solutions to variable-sum games.[17]

[16]McKinsey, *Introduction to the Theory of Games*, p. 332.

[17]For example, it is likely that in retail transactions both retailers and consumers, for the most part, derive benefits. A bibliography of recent work on game theory appears in Luce and Raiffa, *Games and Decisions*, pp. 485–499.

Game theory has been applied very little outside of military problems.[18] The few reports published on the application of game theory shed practically no light on the uses to which the theory has been put in the solution of marketing problems. One source refers briefly to the use of mixed strategies in the timing of advertising but gives no details nor any evaluation of the results. Alderson believes that game theory can be applied to marketing negotiations but does not cite any examples.[19]

Game Theory: Evaluation

Game theory is an analytical method. In one respect it is normative because it seeks to set forth what would constitute rational decisions in specific conflict situations. In another respect it aims to provide a technique for the construction of models of conflict situations. Such models are intended to enable an analyst to predict the gain or loss which would accrue to each of the participants, depending on the strategy choices each made.

Game theory is still in its infancy. It is a static theory that provides unique equilibrium solutions only for the relatively uncomplicated two-person, zero-sum games. For games involving more than two players, whether zero-sum or variable-sum, game theory has had less success in stating what specific outcome will result if the participants make strategy choices in accordance with game theory's concept of rationality.[20]

At present it apparently is not feasible to make firm statements as to the practicability of game theory with respect to models of actual marketing situations without doing a great deal of original research. This is so because the available published information on the application of the theory to marketing situations is meager.

---

[18]Martin Shubik, "The Uses of Game Theory in Management," *Management Science* (October, 1955), pp. 40–54. Game theory is said to have had a profound impact on statistics. See Robert Dorfman, Paul A. Samuelson, and Robert M. Solow, *Linear Programming and Economic Analysis* (New York: McGraw-Hill Book Company, Inc., 1958), p. 417.

[19]Wroe Alderson, *Marketing Behavior and Executive Action* (Homewood, Illinois: Richard D. Irwin, Inc., 1957), pp. 142–43.

[20]The von Neumann-Morgenstern solution to a two-person, variable-sum game amounts to the following: The two players should find a way to play the game so as to maximize the sum of their gains. They should then divide this sum between them in such a way that each gets at least what he could get if he were playing independently but with the other player trying to do him as much harm as possible. Aside from this last condition, the theory offers no way of deciding how the profits will be divided.

The application of the analytical technique of game theory to real-life situations appears to require a good deal of skill and to be fraught with substantial pitfalls. It also requires knowledge of many facts about the situation that may, in fact, not be known. Regardless of whether an analyst intends to use game theory as a normative theory or as a method for predicting the consequences of any of a set of alternative courses of action, it is necessary for him to estimate at least the significant alternative strategies available to the participants and the payoffs associated with combinations of these strategies.

Highly skilled judgments would appear to be necessary in deciding which alternatives are important for the model and the values of the relevant payoffs. Obviously, the need to use judgment in constructing game matrices introduces the possibility of errors that may substantially affect the accuracy of predictions.

Whether difficulties such as these can be successfully met with respect to situations of conflict in marketing cannot be answered now. Only after experience in the application of game theory has accumulated will an answer be forthcoming.

In summary it can be said that normative game theory has not yet been developed to the point where it can designate rational courses of action in game models which constitute abstractions of many real marketing situations. However, game theorists appear to be proceeding in this direction along a road which von Neumann and Morgenstern have asserted is desirable in the development of a theory. That is, they are moving from the analysis of simple to the analysis of the more complicated situations. However, game theory's practicability as a useful analytical tool for marketing situations is not known since the available published information on the use, if any, of the technique in such situations is small.

Since the development of game theory is based so substantially on mathematical methods, it is perhaps appropriate to include the following quotation in these evaluatory comments:

> Mathematics is the study of what is true of hypothetical states of things. That is its essence and definition. Everything in it, therefore, beyond the first precepts for the construction of the hypotheses has to be of the nature of apodictic inference. No doubt, we may reason imperfectly and jump at a conclusion; still, the conclusion so guessed at is, after all, that in a certain supposed state of things something

would necessarily be true. Mathematics is purely hypothetical; it produces nothing but conditional propositions.[21]

A quotation by Williams also appears to be pertinent to an evaluation of game theory:

> . . . Despite current limitations of the theory, perhaps its greatest contribution so far has been an intangible one: the general orientation given to people who are faced with overcomplex problems. Even though these problems are not strictly solvable — certainly at the moment and probably for the indefinite future — it helps to have a framework in which to work on them. The concept of a strategy, the distinctions among players, the role of chance events, the notion of matrix representations of the payoffs, the concepts of pure and mixed strategies, and so on give valuable orientation to persons who must think about complicated conflict situations.[22]

---

[21]Charles S. Pierce, "The Essence of Mathematics," reprinted in Philip P. Wiener (ed.), *Readings in Philosophy of Science* (New York: Charles Scribner's Sons, 1953) p. 11. Pierce's article is from the *Collected Papers of Charles Sanders Pierce*, edited by Charles Hartshorne and Paul Weiss, and published by the Belknap Press of Harvard University.

[22]Williams, *The Compleat Strategyst*, p. 217.

Chapter 5

INTERREGIONAL AND INTRAREGIONAL MARKETING THEORY

During a large part of the more than half century during which the formal study of marketing has developed, economic theory has occupied a central place in the thinking of a number of marketing students. This, of course, is not surprising since marketing is an important aspect of our economy. Moreover, many students of marketing have come to the study of the subject via training in economics.

Among present-day students of marketing, E. T. Grether, of the University of California, is an example of one who attempts to utilize economic theory in the analysis of marketing phenomena.[1] His use of economic theory in marketing is well illustrated by his study of interregional and intraregional marketing.[2]

Grether's Approach to Marketing Theory

Grether's long-time study of marketing literature has led him to conclude that the literature is not short of facts. He is of the opinion that what is needed for the further development of marketing science is: (1) better tools for analyzing the facts of marketing and (2) the development of a conceptual framework that will assist in asking the right questions about marketing phenomena and "in fitting facts into an orderly pattern with enlarged and significant meaning."[3]

---

[1]Other marketing students who take a similar approach are E. R. Hawkins, G. Shepherd, P. J. Verdoorn, and G. Mehren. See, for example, E. R. Hawkins, "Price Policies and Price Theory," *Journal of Marketing*, national quarterly publication of the American Marketing Association, Vol. XVIII (January, 1954), pp. 233–40; G. Shepherd, *Marketing Farm Products — Economic Analysis* (Ames: Iowa State College Press, 1955); P. J. Verdoorn, "Marketing from the Producer's Point of View," *Journal of Marketing*, national quarterly publication of the American Marketing Association, Vol. XX (January, 1956), pp. 221–235; and G. Mehren, "The Theory of the Firm and Marketing," published in Reavis Cox and Wroe Alderson (eds.), *Theory in Marketing* (Homewood, Illinois: Richard D. Irwin, Inc., 1950), pp. 125–142.

[2]In his study of intraregional marketing, Grether focuses on the factors which determine the size of market areas.

[3]E. T. Grether, "A Theoretical Approach to the Analysis of Marketing," published in Reavis Cox and Wroe Alderson (eds.), *Theory in Marketing* (Homewood, Illinois: Richard D. Irwin, Inc., 1950), p. 114.

A desirable ultimate goal for marketing theorists, according to Grether, is the development of applied theory. He does not define the phrase applied theory but distinguishes it from pure theory which he defines as consisting of a logical framework with little or no relevance to reality. In his opinion there is no need for pure theory in marketing.[4] Rather, the development of marketing science will be enhanced if various types of applied theory are developed which would allow:

1. Some direct relationship with important bodies of reality.
2. The preparation and improvement of specific tools (methods) of analysis.
3. The incorporation of individual facts and special bodies of knowledge into a systematic collection of principles and of organized evidence.[5]

In Grether's opinion a marketing theory should be relatively dynamic.[6] Marketing theorists should be willing to sacrifice the perfection of static analysis for the vitality of a strong empirical footing.[7]

Grether believes that marketing science needs to consist of a number of more or less complementary theories or theoretical approaches. A single theory of marketing is not possible, in his opinion, because marketing is too broad and complicated.[8]

Marketing science should be eclectic, according to Grether, using material from other disciplines whenever appropriate. He cites economic theory, group psychology, and ecological studies as possible sources of marketing theory. The interest of the theorizer, he writes, will determine which of the established disciplines will be drawn upon, what data will be relevant, and to what extent new ground must be broken.

---

[4]Grether does not state why he believes that there is no need for pure theory in marketing.

[5]Grether's article in Cox and Alderson (eds.), *op. cit.*, p. 114.

[6]Grether does not define the term dynamic. However, it would appear that he believes that a marketing theory should be such that it takes account of relevant changes in the environment, e.g., developments in human institutions and habits of life, population growth or decline.

[7]This statement seems to imply that the assumptions of static analysis, sometimes or frequently, do not reflect reality. It also appears to imply that theories based on empirical data are likely to generalize more accurately about the facts of marketing life.

[8]When Grether refers to a single theory, he apparently means a general theory which would cover the major aspects of marketing. Multiple theories, on the other hand, would consist of a number of theories, each pertaining only to a particular aspect of marketing. This notion of a marketing science consisting of a number of theories appears to be consistent with Cox's piecemeal approach to the development of marketing science.

Interregional and Intraregional Marketing Theory: Grether's Methodology

In selecting his theoretical approach Grether considered two possibilities: (1) the business policy approach and (2) the economic analysis approach. By the business policy approach Grether means a method of study that "begins with the problems of the individual business enterprise and 'theorizes' about its policy decisions in the field of marketing and selling."[9] This, according to Grether, is the method employed in much of marketing literature. The economic analysis approach, on the other hand, utilizes appropriate elements of economic theory as a springboard for studying various aspects of the behavior of enterprises.

While he finds both of these approaches useful, Grether believes that the economic analysis approach is superior. He criticizes the business policy approach because: "(a) it tends to abstract marketing and selling in an artificial manner from the total behavior of the firm, and (b) . . . it may not produce results that can be linked to a broader body of knowledge."[10] A narrowly conceived business policy approach, he writes, may not even provide a sound basis for policy decisions on the part of the enterprise "since the individual firm is a member of an industry, operates in a given economic region or regions, participates in the broader economy of the United States and the world, and contributes toward and is influenced by broad sets of relationships."[11]

By way of contrast the economic analysis approach, Grether asserts, not only analyzes the behavior of the firm but also facilitates analysis of problems of group adjustment in an industry,[12] in a region, and in an entire economy.[13]

In studying interregional and intraregional marketing Grether begins with relevant portions of economic theory.[14] Then, wherever appropriate, he adjusts this theoretical explanation to fit the facts as revealed by what he terms case materials. That is, he uses economic theory as a framework within which he views the facts of interregional and intraregional marketing.

---

[9]Grether's article in Cox and Alderson (eds.), *op. cit.*, p. 115.

[10]*Ibid.*

[11]*Ibid.*

[12]Economic theory terms this type of analysis "partial equilibrium analysis."

[13]This is termed "general equilibrium analysis" in economic theory.

[14]Grether regards Chamberlain's theory of monopolistic competition as a tentative formulation of a theory of marketing under the highly simplified conditions of the single-product firm selling in a single market directly to buyers without a series of market intermediaries (the marketing channel).

According to Grether it is advantageous for marketing theorists to go beyond economic theory because such study "(a) . . . gives scholars a broad vista, (b) . . . forces them deeper into the stream than might occur otherwise, and (c) the stream flows into a large body of organized knowledge."[15]

Interregional and Intraregional Marketing: Theory Presented by E. T. Grether

Grether's approach to marketing theory is well illustrated by a section which appears in *Marketing in the American Economy*, a basic marketing textbook, coauthored by Grether, Reavis Cox, and Roland S. Vaile.[16] In this section an attempt is made to present an applied theory which explains the operation of interregional marketing and the determination of the market areas of primary producers, manufacturers, wholesalers, and retailers.[17]

Interregional Marketing Theory. Interregional marketing, Grether writes, involves the exchange of goods between economic regions. An economic region is defined:

> . . . as a relatively large geographical area with the following four characteristics: (1) it has more than one center of economic control, (2) it has greater internal homogeneity than would be present if it were merged with other contiguous areas, (3) it exports a characteristic group of products to other areas, and (4) it imports the characteristic products of other areas.[18]

In analyzing marketing in the United States, Grether is unable to identify economic regions using this concept. However, he states that "we know" that economic regions exist. He cites, for example, the New England States, the Pacific Southwest, the Intermountain States, the Pacific Northwest, and the Old South as "regional entities identifiable politically and economically as well as psychologically."[19]

---

[15]Grether's article in Cox and Alderson (eds.), *op. cit.*, p. 116.

[16]R. S. Vaile, E. T. Grether, and R. Cox, *Marketing in the American Economy* (New York: The Ronald Press Company, 1952), pp. 487–569.

[17]Like a coin, Grether's concept of market area has two sides — one refers to selling areas, and the other refers to supply areas.

[18]Grether states that this concept is drawn from Bertil Ohlin, *Interregional and International Trade* (Cambridge: Harvard University Press, 1935).

[19]Vaile, Grether, and Cox, *op. cit.*, p. 489. While these regions do not fit precisely the above concept of an economic region, Grether is willing to accept them as regions apparently because they are widely regarded as such, have usefulness for certain purposes, and can be used as units for the collection of statistics.

The interregional marketing theory presented by Grether predicts that goods will be exchanged among regions if there are effective reciprocal demands for the products of the regions and if there are opportunities for trading gains. The basis for trade provided by these conditions may be either absolute or comparative. An absolute basis for trade exists when consumers residing in one region desire goods which cannot be produced locally but which can be purchased from other regions. A comparative basis for trade exists among regions when there are regional differences in costs, prices, sales facilities, and products.

Under conditions of pure competition, Grether writes, goods would move between regions only if there were price differences large enough to cover trading and handling costs and necessary profits.[20] Marketing under these conditions would ultimately result in price differences between the trading regions which differed only by the amount of transfer costs. This result would materialize, according to the theory, because demand would expand in the exporting region, thus raising prices there. In the importing region prices would drop because of increased supplies.

Grether writes, however, that marketing in the United States is not conducted under conditions of pure competition. Products marketed interregionally are frequently not homogeneous. Rather, many of them have been differentiated through brand promotion and by other factors. Product differentiation, Grether writes, enables essentially similar products to be exchanged among regions even when prices in these regions are virtually the same. This exchange will take place, he states, to satisfy consumer preferences.

Whereas under pure competition interregional marketers will not sell unless they can recover transportation costs, in the real world of heterogeneous competition, Grether writes, sellers may be willing to absorb these costs or the economies of enlarging the scale of production may offset them. Sellers may, moreover, be able to recover these costs through price discrimination[21] if demand elasticities vary among pur-

---

[20]Necessary profits, in the theory of pure competition, means profits large enough to induce businessmen to continue to perform, or to undertake, business activities.

[21]The authors of one textbook in economic theory state that price discrimination "occurs when a monopolist charges different prices for different units of a commodity, even though these units are in fact homogeneous so far as their physical nature is concerned." See Alfred W. Stonier and Douglas C. Hague, A Textbook of Economic Theory (3rd ed.; New York: Longmans, Green & Co., Inc., 1955), p. 172.

chasing regions.[22] These facts of marketing life, according to Grether, require appropriate modification of the purely competitive theory of interregional marketing.

In further elaboration of this theory, he writes that the lowering of commodity prices in the importing region will tend to make production of the imported products even less desirable and enlarge the necessity for imports. With respect to the exporting region, the theory states that the rising prices for export products will tend to attract capital and labor into the output of these goods. Eventually the basis of interregional trade will be enlarged by a growth in the original inequality of factoral supplies out of which trade developed.[23]

The volume of goods marketed interregionally is stated by the theory to depend primarily on four factors:

1. The relative inequality of regions with respect to supplies of factors of production. Regions will tend to export products they can produce by using resources that are abundant and cheap within their boundaries.

2. The relative prosperity of regions. Other things being equal, the theory states, regions with high total and per capita incomes will tend to generate more trade than poor regions.

3. The strength of the reciprocal demands among regions. There will be a larger total volume of trade if two trading regions have a strong demand for each other's characteristic products.

4. The relative effectiveness of internal competition. The theory reasons that the basis for interregional marketing "should normally be stronger when competition within regions is active and effective."[24]

All the regions that participate in interregional marketing gain advantages according to the theory. However, these gains are not divided equally among all the trading regions. To the extent that interregional trade arises out of an absolute basis of trade, every region's pattern of living is enriched by having available for consumption a variety of products which would otherwise be unobtainable. Insofar as this trade arises out of differences in cost and price, the income of all

---

[22]Vaile, Grether, and Cox, *op. cit.*, p. 493. The way in which businessmen are able to charge higher prices for the same physical product in different regions when elasticities of demand are different is discussed in *ibid.*, pp. 173–181. See also, Sidney Weintraub, *Price Theory* (New York: Pitman Publishing Corp., 1949), pp. 311–16.

[23]Vaile, Grether, and Cox, *op. cit.*, pp. 501–03.

[24]R. S. Vaile, E. T. Grether, and R. Cox, *Marketing in the American Economy* (New York: The Ronald Press Company, 1952), p. 509.

trading regions is said to be increased and the general level of living raised by the economies produced by regional specialization.[25]

Public and private barriers to interregional trade, according to Grether, operate to negate the validity of this theory of interregional marketing. With these barriers in effect, trade no longer follows the "normal" dictates of reciprocal demand and competitive costs and prices. Institutional inertia, according to Grether, also interferes for a time with the "normal" operation of interregional marketing as described by the theory. Trade between regions does not immediately adjust itself to changes in conditions. He cites as an example the possibility that a region may hold markets for a considerable period after conditions have changed while capital is being divested in one area and invested in another.

Intraregional Marketing Theory. In developing his applied theory of market areas, Grether attempts to ascertain what factors influence the size of these areas and the effect each has on the dimensions of a market area. He states that the problems involved are enormously complicated, and for this reason he begins the development of his applied theory with simplifying assumptions that lead him into what he terms the elementary theory of market area determination.

The simplest case he presents assumes that all the buyers of a given commodity are distributed evenly along a straight line of finite length, that they all have equal and uniform demands, and that there exists only one seller. It is, moreover, assumed that this seller is able to locate at any point on the line. If it is assumed, Grether writes, that this seller wishes to maximize his net revenue, he would locate at the center of the line. He would make this decision because from this location both his sales at a given price and his net revenue would be at a maximum.

Grether's analysis is portrayed in Figure 7.[26] This diagram shows how the cost to different consumers and the volume purchased by different consumers would vary in his assumed situation.

AB is the line along which buyers are spaced uniformly, the seller being located at its midpoint S. Grether calls ST and ST' transfer

---

[25]The gains from interregional marketing would be divided equally among participating regions if, as a result of interregional marketing, each region improved its levels of living to the same extent.

[26]This figure appears in Vaile, Grether and Cox, *op. cit.*, p. 515.

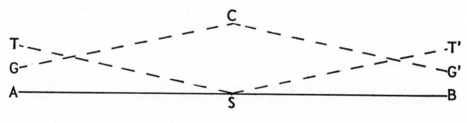

Figure 7

TRANSFER GRADIENTS AND CONSUMPTION GRADIENTS IN A STRAIGHT-LINE MARKET

Source: R. S. Vaile, E. T. Grether, and R. Cox, *Marketing in the American Economy* (New York: The Ronald Press, 1952), p. 515.

gradients. *ST* and *ST'* are drawn on the assumption that transfer costs increase in direct proportion to distance. *CG* and *CG'* are termed consumption gradients. They are drawn so that they show that purchases are largest at the location of the seller and fall off in either direction as spatial costs rise. *CG* and *CG'* are drawn on the assumption that the decrease in consumer purchases is directly proportional to the increase in costs.

Grether also predicts the location of a seller in a situation where buyers are located uniformly in a two-dimensional plane. He, moreover, describes the conical form of transfer and consumption gradients in such an assumed situation. In this instance the seller would be located at the center of a circle.

Further on in his analysis, Grether complicates the market situation by assuming that a rival seller appears. This second seller offers an identical product and price. Where would each of these two sellers locate, and how would they divide the market between them? If the first seller took a position one quarter of the distance from one end of the line and the second seller took a position one quarter of the distance from the other end of the line, each would share the market equally. Grether points out, however, that either seller could get a larger share of the market by moving towards the other, unless the other retaliated. For this reason the only stable solution to this problem is for the two to locate themselves side by side at the center of the line. Under the conditions assumed, he states, each seller would receive one half of the business. Consumers would be indifferent as to which seller they patronized, and the allocation of their trade would be determined by chance. This type of problem would, according to Grether, "become increasingly complicated and interesting as more sellers joined it."[27]

From his analysis Grether develops what he calls "a principle for the real world." He states this principle as follows:

> Under conditions of pure competition, when demand is uniformly dispersed through space, and location is free instead of fixed,[28] sellers would become so diffused through space as to provide each with an equal and uniform market for a given product.[29] The principle of spatial decentralization and diffusion in marketing would appear to be fundamental in any endeavor to minimize the costs of transfer.[30]

Grether asserts that concentration and centralization can arise only out of conditions differing from the assumptions of his hypothetical situation. The concentration of demand at a few points and the presence of important economies of scale in production would, he states, introduce significant variations.[31]

In the two situations discussed above, Grether assumed that the sellers were free to locate wherever they wished in a straight-line market. His next step in developing what he calls the elementary theory of market determination is to assume that sellers have fixed locations. Figure 8 illustrates his reasoning in this hypothetical situation.

In Figure 8, A and B represent the two sellers. In this instance Grether assumes that each seller is selling an identical product and that transfer costs vary directly with distance. If the vendors' selling prices were identical, they would divide the market equally; and XY (a straight line) would show the division of the market. However, if it is assumed that selling prices at the two selling points are unequal, the boundary line between the market areas of the two selling centers would take the form of a hyperbola.[32] According to Grether buyers on

---

[27]*Ibid.*

[28]In this context location is said to be fixed when locational movement is not free but involves costs.

[29]Grether does not state how the number of sellers is determined.

[30]Vaile, Grether, and Cox, *op. cit.*, p. 516.

[31]Vaile, Grether, and Cox, *op. cit.*, p. 516. This appears to be a curious use of the notion of "a principle for the real world." Grether's assumptions and resultant principle, as he states, refer to conditions of pure competition. He apparently is explaining the concentration and centralization of sellers which is observed in the real world by pointing out that the conditions of the real world differ from his purely competitive assumptions.

[32]In Figure 8, EF and CD are drawn so that at any point on either curve the cost of a product purchased from seller A, i.e., selling price plus transfer costs, equals the cost of purchasing the same product from seller B. Under the conditions assumed for Figure 8, both vendors are selling the identical product, and transfer costs vary directly with

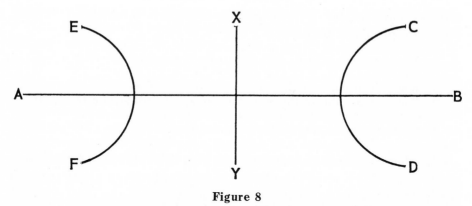

Figure 8

MARKET AREAS WHERE PRICES ARE UNEQUAL

Source: R. S. Vaile, E. T. Grether, and R. Cox, *Marketing in the American Economy* (New York: The Ronald Press, 1952), p. 518.

this curve will be indifferent as to whether they purchase from one center or another. Buyers on either side of the curve will purchase from the center on that side.

In discussing the above theoretical method, Grether states:

> It would be possible to elaborate the formal abstract theory of market area determination by enlarging the number of sellers and the number of competing market centers, or by varying the assumptions. Students with a flair for geometric patterns will find this an illuminating exercise. The potentialities for useful mental exercise are tremendous, as the number of competing centers and the variety of conditions increase. A solution is always possible so long as (1) products and sellers are assumed to be homogeneous, (2) prices are quoted at the location of the seller, and (3) transfer costs follow a determinate pattern.[33]

Market Area Determination: Primary Producers

Grether asserts that the elementary theory of market area determination under pure competition can be applied to the real world with

---

distance. Curves *EF* and *CD* are illustrative hyperbolas. Thus in the situation assumed in Figure 8, the curve dividing the market areas of the two selling centers would be either a straight line if each vendor sold his product at the same price or a hyperbola if each vendor sold at a different price. If seller *A* was able to sell his product at a lower price or had a transfer cost advantage, the boundary of his market area might be *CD*. Similarly, *EF* might divide the market area between *A* and *B* if the latter could sell his product at a lower price or had a transfer cost advantage.

[33]Vaile, Grether, and Cox, *op. cit.*, p. 518. Grether states that the simple theory of market area determination is also applicable to the supply side.

the least modification in the marketing of primary products. This is so, he states, primarily because:

1. After they are graded, primary products are approximately homogeneous.
2. They are usually provided by numerous producers.
3. The specific value of these products is sufficiently low for transport costs to exercise a significant influence on market outreach.
4. Administered pricing is almost nonexistent.

Grether's applied theory of market area determination for primary products asserts that in the absence of governmental or group controls the distances primary products will move to market and the volume of movement will be determined largely by the amount of transport a given level and elasticity of demand will cover. However, simple calculations of price and distance, he states, will not provide the answer. This is so, Grether explains, because actual freight rates depart widely from what they would be if based strictly upon distance, weight, and cost. Market equalization, blanketing, in-transit privileges, and discrimination in favor of particular products modify the structure substantially.

Although Grether asserts the validity of this theory, he cautions that, in addition to broad general principles, an adequate knowledge of the manner in which primary product market areas are determined must also include information about many special factors including variations in the quality of goods produced in different regions. He also warns that the factors involved in the determination of market areas, e.g., demand and supply, are subject to dynamic forces and that established market areas do change over a period of time.[34]

Market Area Determination: Manufacturers

In developing his applied theory of market area determination for manufactured goods, Grether has concluded that the principles of market area determination under pure competition have practically no applicability to these products. Six factors, he writes, are principal determinants of such areas:

1. The degree of product differentiation and the relative effectiveness of brand promotion.

---

[34]Grether does not relate his interregional and intraregional marketing theories.

2. The range of price choices in administered pricing made possible by product differentiation, oligopoly, or other influences.
3. The ratio of fixed to total costs.
4. The economies of scale of production at each center.
5. The burden of transfer costs in total delivered prices to customers.
6. The radius of economical outreach.[35]

Grether's theory predicts that a manufacturer with marked differentiation of his product and brand, a high proportion of fixed costs, large economies of scale, and low transfer costs percentagewise will try to sell over wide areas, i.e., in regional, national, or world markets. The market areas of such competing manufacturers, he states, overlap and may even overlap completely; in cases such as these it is not possible to discover sharp breaking points. In this connection Grether writes that although market areas overlap partially or completely, there are almost always differences among manufacturers in the relative strength of their penetration.

In the case of products for which transfer costs are important percentagewise and economies of scale do not offset full freight absorption, Grether predicts that manufacturers will face economic obstacles to enlarging their market outreach. Such manufacturers may decide to limit their market area, or they may enlarge their market area by (1) establishing branch plants or (2) reducing the burden of freight absorption by adopting zone or basing-point pricing.

Grether asserts that where numerous manufacturers sell a homogeneous product the elementary theory of market area determination is applicable. Product homogeneity, he states, makes for relatively sharp breaking points between market areas of sellers located at different points. Where a product is homogeneous but the number of manufacturers selling the product are few, however, Grether predicts that overlapping of market areas will result. He states that such manufacturers are likely to seek to enlarge their market areas by quoting uniform delivered prices or multiple basing-point prices.

Market Area Determination: Wholesalers

Grether's analysis of the determination of wholesale market areas leads him to conclude that the principles of selling-area determination under pure competition apply "quite directly" to wholesaling; that is,

---

[35]Vaile, Grether, and Cox, *op. cit.*, p. 526.

selling price and transfer costs are important determinants of wholesale selling areas. He cautions, however, that allowance must be made for various special circumstances.

The principal wholesale market area determining factors which he includes in these special circumstances are kinds of goods handled,[36] kinds of enterprises,[37] comparative prices, transfer costs, and the physiography of the surrounding territory.[38]

Grether states that wholesale selling areas tend to be narrow for staple standardized products, e.g., sugar, flour, and tobacco. By way of contrast, he states, specialty goods, particularly those of high specific value, often are sold by wholesalers over wide trading areas. The wholesale selling areas for shopping goods also tend to be relatively large. According to Grether one device available to a wholesaler who wants to expand his market area is the broadening of his product line.

Another such technique, according to Grether, is product differentiation which may be based on the offering of unique products, the use of private brands, or the establishment of exclusive distributorships. "When wholesale trading areas show little resemblance to the pattern of simple theoretical cases," Grether writes, "the reason almost invariably lies in some form of product differentiation."[39]

Grether lacks evidence for generalization, but he reasons that comparative prices are important in determining the areal outreach of competing wholesale centers and enterprises. This is so, he says, because wholesalers deal with business, institutional, and governmental buyers. Since these institutions are generally concerned about price, a comparatively low price at one wholesale center may be expected to push the breaking point toward competing centers.

Grether also points to the influence of terrain on wholesale selling areas. Terrain is a significant factor, he states, because it influences the character and cost of transportation facilities, the location of industry, and the distribution and density of population. Among the other factors which Grether lists as affecting the size of wholesale selling areas are the human factors of personality, drive, and initiative.

------

[36]Here Grether is referring to staples, specialty products, shopping goods, and the width and depth of a wholesaler's assortment.

[37]Types of wholesalers, e.g., cash and carry wholesalers and service wholesalers.

[38]Grether states that a number of geographic factors influence the size of market areas of wholesalers, e.g., location on a seacoast or the mouth of a large river, nearness to mountains, deserts, etc.

[39]Vaile, Grether, and Cox, op. cit., p. 542.

Market Area Determination: Retailers

Grether's study of retail selling areas has led him to conclude that the problem of ascertaining the factors which determine such areas is one of the most complex aspects of spatial competition. He writes that sharp boundaries between retail enterprises and retail centers are rare, if they occur at all. Invariably, Grether states, between competing retail enterprises and retail centers there is some overlapping of market areas derived from differences in assortment, service, price, traffic flow, and other pertinent factors. He writes that the nature of the overlapping and the extent of the outreach cannot be predicted in general terms. As a consequence, he states, each enterprise and center must make its own analysis of the particular factors that delineate its selling area.[40]

Many factors, according to Grether, influence the size of retail selling areas. The kind of product handled is one of these. In the main, he states, the selling areas for specialty and shopping goods are larger than those for convenience goods.

Whereas Grether found that prices and transport costs were especially important in determining the selling areas of primary products, wholesalers, and some homogeneous manufactured goods, these factors, he states, have less significance with respect to retail selling areas. In general, Grether writes, price is more important as a factor influencing the selling areas of individual firms than as an influence upon market areas of retail centers. He predicts that a retail enterprise that markedly cuts the prices of known brands will enlarge its area of patronage unless its price cuts are met by competitors. In contrast, Grether states, uniformity of prices on known merchandise operates to reduce the selling areas of retailers.

Grether lists several other factors which influence the size of retail selling areas. Those that he mentions are automobile ownership,

----

[40]The concept of a retail selling area has not been developed to the point where one concept is widely accepted among marketing students. Some students, for example, think of a retail selling area as one from which a retail center or enterprise draws its sales. In contrast, other students view a retail selling area as an area from which a retail center or enterprise draws more than 50 per cent of its sales. Somewhat related to this question is the question of where retail sales are consummated. For statistical purposes they are usually counted as taking place at the location of a retail enterprise. However, this is misleading since a significant portion of retail sales is completed at places of business or homes, e.g., door-to-door sales. Another conceptual problem that arises in this connection is what is the location of the consumer. For statistical purposes the consumer is frequently counted as being located at his place of residence. However, consumers spend much of their time elsewhere and not infrequently make retail purchases in areas distant from their homes, e.g., purchases made by individuals in neighborhoods where they are employed.

geography of an area, communication facilities available to retailers, nonmerchandise attractions of trading centers, attraction of outstanding merchandise institutions, and the effectiveness of retailer group action.

Automobile ownership can either operate to enlarge retail selling areas or to reduce them. They produce the former effect by enabling consumers to travel longer distances to shop. The reverse occurs when extensive automobile use produces traffic congestion and creates parking problems. Geography may influence the size of selling areas if the topography is such as to hem in the retailers of a particular trading center. Grether cites Berkeley, California, as an example of a city which has per capita retail sales much smaller than those of other cities which have a comparable size but are less closely hemmed in by topography and competition.

The availability of communication facilities, of course, enables retailers to reach out and influence consumers located at a distance from their establishment. Nonmerchandise attractions of trading centers such as theaters, medical facilities, and banks operate to enlarge retail selling areas because they draw consumers to a city from the surrounding area. Grether cites Marshall Field and Company in Chicago as an example of an outstanding merchandising institution which contributes to the enlargement of the selling area of other retailers by attracting consumers. Another device available to retailers for enlarging their market area, Grether states, is group action by all merchants in planning and promotion.

Evaluation of Theories Presented by Grether

It will be recalled that Grether has expressed specific views as to the form that the development of marketing theory and science should take. His views can be summarized succinctly as follows:

1. It is desirable to develop a conceptual framework within which the facts of marketing can be organized.
2. Marketing theory should be dynamic and should have some direct relationship with important bodies of reality (applied theory). Marketing has no need for static pure theory.

In pursuance of these goals Grether has used a combination of economic theory, the tools of economic analysis, and the results of empirical investigation in developing theories of interregional and intra-regional marketing.

The theory of interregional marketing presented by Grether is a modified version of the purely competitive theory of interregional trade. It is modified by such factors as successfully differentiated products and political and private barriers to interregional marketing.

It is difficult to make a judgment as to the extent to which this theory is, using Grether's terminology, pure or applied theory. This is so because the theory is largely a logical explanation developed from assumptions.[41] While Grether has injected into the explanation certain facts characteristic of an economy of heterogeneous competition, the theory, nevertheless, essentially asserts that conclusions logically derived from assumptions explain the reality of interregional marketing. This may be completely true, only partly true, or largely false. Since Grether does not substantiate the theory with data, the extent to which it is pure or applied cannot be stated.

The conceptual framework presented by Grether, however, appears useful to any analysis of interregional marketing from the social point of view. This is so because it focuses attention on such questions as:

1. The circumstances which may give rise to interregional marketing.
2. The effect of interregional marketing on regional prices and the products offered for sale by regions.
3. The effect of sales promotion on trade between regions.
4. The economic consequences to society and specific regions of interregional marketing.

In developing theory pertaining to market area determination, Grether started by assuming pure competition and then, for simple cases, conceptually delineated market areas of competing sellers. Price and transfer costs were the prime determinants of market areas in this framework. However, Grether, in effect, made very little use of this approach as he penetrated into his analysis of the market areas of sellers other than primary producers.[42] Since marketing institutions in the United States operate under conditions of heterogeneous competition, Grether was, of course, realistic in doing this. However, in view of the fact that pure competition is rare in United States marketing, it is perplexing that he included this type of theory at all.

Some theorists utilize pure theory as a desirable standard. Thus,

---

[41]Grether defines pure theory as consisting of a logical framework with little or no relevance to reality. By applied theory he apparently means pure theory modified, more or less, by the facts of marketing life. It would seem that Grether would not view a theory as pure merely by virtue of the fact that it is a logical framework. If such a theory also had little or no relevance to reality, he would presumably place it in the pure theory category.

[42]It will be recalled that even with respect to primary producers Grether emphasized that specific circumstances, such as important product quality differences, might diminish the significance of price and transfer costs in the determination of selling areas.

some economic theorists use the purely competitive theory of price to support a thesis that monopolistic competition is undesirable because it results in higher prices and unused productive capacity and labor. Others use pure theory as a starting point for explaining reality, gradually relaxing assumptions so as to develop a theory which more nearly explains reality. Grether apparently desires to use pure theory for this latter purpose. As his theoretical analysis of market areas ultimately developed, however, it appears that his use of pure competition as a springboard in this regard had little utility.

Grether's theory of market area determination can be termed a qualitative presentation of the many factors which play a role in the determination of market areas. Certain of these factors tend to enlarge market areas; whereas, others operate to diminish the size of a market area. Which factors are more important than others, however, are not stated by the theory; and the theory could not be used to predict the boundaries of any particular market area.

This theory, however, is illuminating because it states in general terms the effect of the numerous factors involved in the determination of market areas. Moreover, it contributes to understanding by revealing the differences in the kinds of factors which are important in the determination of the market areas of various types of sellers.

It is probably correct to say that, in its present form, Grether's theory of market area determination represents a good beginning toward the ultimate development of a more useful and informative theory. The fact that the present theory is qualitative leaves vague the relative importance of market area determining factors and gives the theory only limited predictive value. Grether's analysis appears to have particular usefulness as a framework which focuses attention on the major determinants of market areas.

This appraisal of the theories presented by Grether reveals the following conclusions as to the extent that Grether has attained his theoretical objectives:

1. Grether contributes useful conceptual frameworks for a social analysis of interregional marketing and for analyses of individual market areas.
2. In the absence of substantiating data the extent to which the theory of interregional marketing presented by Grether is pure or applied is not known.
3. Grether's theory of market area determination, while enlightening, needs to be developed further with the objective of making it less qualitative.

Chapter **6**

MARKETING FUNCTIONS

Background

The functional approach to the study of marketing is regarded by many marketing students as a major tool of analysis.[1] It has occupied an important place in marketing literature since 1912 when it was first introduced by Arch W. Shaw, a pioneer marketing analyst.[2]

The functional approach is termed an approach because it focuses on one of several aspects of marketing. The authors of one textbook describe the nature of the functional approach as follows:

> Marketing functions are homogeneous groups of activities which are necessary to the performance of the general function of distribution. Thus marketing comes to be defined as a process of exchange involving a series of activities necessary to the movement of goods or services into consumption. Functional analysis calls attention to the basic nature of these operations.[3]

Other approaches used in the study of marketing are the institutional, commodity, historical, cost and legal approaches.

In addition to Shaw, two other early students of marketing functions were L. D. H. Weld and P. T. Cherington. Whereas Shaw's original analysis centered on the "functions of middlemen,"[4] Weld, writing in 1917, spoke of "marketing functions."[5] Weld justified his position by stating that the functions were not always performed by

---

[1] P. D. Converse, H. W. Huegy, and R. V. Mitchell, *The Elements of Marketing* (6th ed.; New York: Prentice Hall, Inc., 1958), p. 117.

[2] Arch W. Shaw, "Some Problems in Market Distribution," *Quarterly Journal of Economics* (August, 1912), pp. 703–75. This article was later reprinted in book form as A. W. Shaw, *Some Problems in Market Distribution* (Cambridge: Harvard University Press, 1915).

[3] Edward A. Duddy and David A. Revzan, *Marketing: An Institutional Approach* (2nd ed.; New York: McGraw-Hill Book Company, Inc., 1953), pp. 20–21.

[4] He listed these functions as: sharing the risk, transporting the goods, financing the operations, selling (communication of ideas about goods), assembling, assorting, and reshipping.

[5] L. D. H. Weld, "Marketing Functions and Mercantile Organization," *American Economic Review* (June, 1917), pp. 306–18.

middlemen but were often performed to a greater or lesser extent by producers and consumers.[6] Writing several years later, Cherington emphasized the fruitfulness of the functional approach as compared with the study of marketing agencies. His position was that agencies are constantly changing; whereas, functions are inherent in any marketing system.[7]

Since the introduction of the functional approach in 1912, marketing functions have been subjected to much study. These numerous studies, however, have given rise to a good deal of confusion which can be attributed to the large diversity of concepts of marketing functions and to the many differences among the activities which authors have labeled marketing functions. Some marketing students list only four or five marketing functions; others list seven or eight; and others list a larger number.[8] Evidence of the wide diversity prevalent in the analysis of marketing functions was revealed in a study conducted by F. W. Ryan. Ryan studied numerous written materials involving functional analysis; and on the basis of information extracted from these sources, he drew up a list of 16 functional categories and 120 functional elements.[9]

Robert Bartels, who made an extensive study of marketing literature published prior to 1940, has written that the variety of functional analyses found in marketing literature stems from the fact that different authors differ in their concepts of marketing, in their points of view, and in their methodology for analyzing functions. "Variations in the writers' fundamental assumptions," he writes, "or in their tools of analysis naturally lead to variations in the products of their thinking."[10] While Bartels' comments are no doubt valid, it should be noted that

---

[6]Weld defined marketing functions as the services that must be performed in getting commodities from producer to consumer. His list of marketing functions included: assembling, storing, assumption of risks, financing, rearrangement (sorting, grading, breaking bulk, packaging, etc.), selling, and transportation.

[7]See Paul T. Cherington, *The Elements of Marketing* (New York: The Macmillan Company, 1920).

[8]Brief descriptions of the development of the functional approach are included in the following articles: F. W. Ryan, "Functional Elements of Market Distribution," *Harvard Business Review* (January, 1935), pp. 205–24; E. S. Fullbrook, "The Functional Concept in Marketing," *Journal of Marketing* (January, 1940), pp. 229–37; and Edmund D. McGarry, "Some Functions of Marketing Reconsidered," published in Reavis Cox and Wroe Alderson (eds.), *Theory in Marketing* (Homewood, Illinois: Richard D. Irwin, Inc., 1950), pp. 263–79.

[9]Ryan, "Functional Elements of Market Distribution," p. 214. A functional element, according to Ryan, is a single marketing activity, while a functional category is a term which encompasses more than one functional element. He writes: "Selling, for example, may be considered as a functional category, while transporting and storage are merely functional elements belonging in the category of handling or merchandising."

[10]Robert Bartels, "Marketing Literature — Development and Appraisal" (Ph.D. dissertation, Ohio State University, 1941), p. 160.

variation in lists of marketing functions has also been due to differences in the explicit or implicit purposes of various authors who have set down classifications of marketing functions.

During the period since World War II, the subject of marketing functions has come under additional analysis and elaboration, especially by Edmund D. McGarry. McGarry has worked on developing a theory of marketing based on an analysis of marketing functions.

McGarry's Approach to Marketing Theory

McGarry's interest in marketing theory and science has extended over more than three decades. During this period his thoughts on the nature of marketing theory and the practicability of developing such theory have apparently undergone some change.

In an article published in 1936, McGarry wrote that the scientific method involved four steps:

1. Selection of facts.
2. Registration of these facts.
3. Rearrangement of the facts into some workable form, to bring order out of chaos.
4. Finding a formula or a conclusion.[11]

McGarry regarded such formulas or conclusions as scientific laws. He stated that they are laws in the sense of probabilities rather than in the sense of something that is absolutely certain and unvarying. At the time he wrote this article, McGarry appeared to be impressed with the utility of multiple correlation analysis in developing scientific laws.[12]

McGarry's recent writings, however, reflect pessimism as to the practicability of developing such scientific laws. The reason for this, he states, is that most of the important factors are difficult to define and impossible to measure. He has also expressed the opinion that:

> . . . the development of a science of marketing is more likely to come from seeking out new theories — broad conceptual schemes — than from attempting to collect bits and pieces of so-called principles. A tenable conceptual scheme would indicate the causal, conditional, and

---

[11]Writers on scientific method do not maintain that there is only one scientific method. One such writer states: "Scientific method is a collective term denoting the various processes by the aid of which the sciences are built up. In a wide sense, any mode of investigation by which scientific or other impartial and systematic knowledge is acquired is called a scientific method." *The Encyclopedia Britannica* (14th ed.; New York: Encyclopedia Britannica, Inc.), Vol. 20 (1951), p.127.

[12]Edmund D. McGarry, "The Importance of Scientific Method in Advertising," *Journal of Marketing*, national quarterly publication of the American Marketing Association, Vol. I (October, 1936), pp. 84–86.

influential relationships among the innumerable factors involved in [a marketing phenomenon] such as advertising.[13]

Writing in 1953, McGarry expressed the view that marketing students were dealing only with the incipient stages of theory formation. He wrote:

> At this stage the thinking is more in the nature of conjecture, inference and speculation about the facts we already know than in the collection and analysis of new facts.[14]

McGarry defines theory as a "general principle offered to explain marketing phenomena."[15] The steps that need to be followed, according to McGarry, in the development and acceptance of a marketing theory are:

1. The initial statement of a theory represents speculation and conjecture about a body of facts.
2. Such a theory must then be subjected to certain questions such as: Does the theory make sense? Is the formulation consistent throughout? Theories have to be subjected to the most rigid criticism by the competent scholars in the field.
3. A theory should then be scrutinized as to whether it fits the facts. Most theories will have to go through a process of modification before they will be acceptable.
4. Along with the tests of logic and realism, a theory should be subjected to other tests such as: Does the theory contribute anything to our understanding and insight? Is it merely play-logic, or does it reach down into fundamental issues?
5. Does the theory lead to further questioning and thinking about the subject?[16]

Developing marketing theories in this way will, according to McGarry, involve many conflicts of judgment and opinion. He writes:

> . . . but the ultimate result should be carefully reasoned and carefully refined concepts which will fit the situations as we know them and aid

---

[13]Edmund D. McGarry, "Dean Lockley's Advertising Principles," *Journal of Marketing*, national quarterly publication of the American Marketing Association, Vol. XIX (April, 1955), p. 352. In this note McGarry asserts his inclination to agree with the following statement by James B. Conant: "Only in very recent times did science emerge from the other human activities which had been accumulating knowledge for thousands of years. . . . The revolutionary advances in science are made in terms of new conceptual schemes, not in improved methods, and not in terms of amassing data. . . . When new conceptual schemes emerge, a whole series of phenomena tend to fall into line or are explained by the new theory."

[14]Edmund D. McGarry, "Some New Viewpoints in Marketing," *Journal of Marketing*, national quarterly publication of the American Marketing Association, Vol. XVIII (July, 1953), p. 40.

[15]*Ibid.*, p. 33. McGarry does not define what he means by the words "principle," "explain," and "phenomena."

[16]*Ibid.*, p. 40.

in explaining what is happening. Out of all this groping to find explanations should eventually come a body of tested theories which will help answer some of the critical marketing problems of the day.[17]

McGarry's Analysis of Marketing Functions

Macroscopic Functional Analysis. McGarry's study of marketing functions constitutes his effort to formulate a theory of marketing.[18] His analysis does not focus on the activities of specific marketing agencies but, rather, takes a macroscopic view. He thinks of marketing as a basic component unit of an economy which facilitates the adjustment of man and his environment. Marketing agencies facilitate this adjustment by maintaining contact between producing agencies and consumers, and performing functions which enable consumers to fill their needs from among products mass produced by industry.

These agencies, McGarry thinks, constantly search for and select products which can be offered to consumers and, thus, modify the products which are made. Through their efforts to persuade consumers to take the products which are produced, they condition peoples' likes and dislikes; through their pricing methods, they adjust the costs of making and distributing products to what consumers can afford to spend; and through their storing and transporting of products, they adjust the times when they can be consumed and the places where they will be consumed. These fundamental activities performed by marketing institutions are termed the functions of marketing by McGarry.[19]

Not only does functional analysis reveal the *raison d'etre* of marketing, according to McGarry, but it is useful for another reason. By breaking the marketing process down into its functions, it is possible to separate the essential from the nonessential elements. Functional analysis, he writes, should permit an analyst to evaluate the activities that are performed in terms of ultimate objectives and to ascertain those that are necessary and those that are not. McGarry asserts that through the study of functions changes in the structure of marketing

---

[17]*Ibid.* This statement appears to imply that a theory is formulated by a process of speculative logical reasoning.

[18]He was led to this effort by his conclusion that existing analyses of how individuals selected the products they bought and how those products were made to conform to what people wanted seemed "confused, inconsistent and superficial." See Edmund D. McGarry, "Some New Viewpoints in Marketing," *Journal of Marketing,* national quarterly publication of the American Marketing Association, Vol. XVIII (July, 1953), pp. 38–39.

[19]*Ibid.,* p. 39. The term "function," according to McGarry, should be restricted to the *sine qua non* of marketing, i.e., those things without which marketing would not exist. See also McGarry, "Some Functions of Marketing Reconsidered," published in Cox and Alderson (eds.), *Theory in Marketing,* p. 268.

caused by shifting, combining, or eliminating activities from one agency to another should be made understandable.

McGarry includes the following six activities in his formal list of marketing functions:

1. *Contactual function:* the process of searching out the market. In the American economy it consists of finding out either who the potential buyers are or who the potential sellers are, where they are located, and how they can be reached.
2. *Propaganda function:* includes all the methods used by the seller to influence people to buy from him and all the methods used by the buyer to induce sellers to sell to him.
3. *Merchandising function:* includes all the adjustments made in the goods and in their presentation to meet the needs and desires of potential consumers or users. It includes quality determination as well as measurement, packaging, branding, and display at strategic points to stimulate consumer interest.
4. *Physical distribution function:* includes transportation and storage.
5. *Pricing function:* involves the selection of a price high enough to make production possible and low enough to induce users to accept the goods.
6. *Termination function:* includes determination of terms of sale for each specific transaction including delivery dates, credit arrangements, guarantees, service policies, the carrying out of the bargain, and the adjustment of complaints.[20]

As McGarry views our marketing system, the merchandising and propaganda functions are believed to be "co-ordinate in adjusting products to their prospective users, on the one hand, and in adjusting potential users to the products made for them, on the other."[21]

From this general treatment of marketing functions, McGarry has gone on to a detailed analysis of the propaganda and contactual functions.

The Propaganda Function. In discussing the propaganda function, McGarry concentrates his discussion on advertising. He thinks of advertising as a type of propaganda which attempts to condition people to act in a way favorable to the propagandist. Advertising, McGarry asserts, is used primarily by sellers to obtain a market by conditioning people to accept the particular products offered.[22]

---

[20]Edmund D. McGarry, "Some Functions of Marketing Reconsidered," published in Reavis Cox and Wroe Alderson (eds.), *Theory in Marketing* (Homewood, Illinois: Richard D. Irwin, Inc., 1950), pp. 269–273.

[21]*Ibid.*, p. 273.

[22]Edmund D. McGarry, "The Propaganda Function in Marketing," *Journal of Marketing,* national quarterly publication of the American Marketing Association, Vol. XXIII (October, 1958), p. 131.

He believes that advertising has to take a substantial part of the responsibility for making sales. This is so because: "To a great extent salesmen, particularly at the retail level, have become anonymous persons — unknown either to the selling firm or to the buyer — who merely facilitate the sale by formally presenting the product and accepting payment."[23] As a consequence, the task of adjusting the consumer to the product is done by the "mass propaganda" called advertising.

McGarry believes that for advertising to be effective copy must be expressed in terms in which the consumer thinks. Advertising must recognize, McGarry says, that ". . . the consumer . . . is but imperfectly rational, and that he hates the labor of rational thinking, and that he is sometimes more impressed by what seems to others to be superficial than by the real merits of the products."[24]

McGarry discusses rational versus emotional appeals in advertising messages. Despite the fact that he regards the consumer as imperfectly rational, he does not reject the possible sales-building effectiveness of rational appeals. He does think, however, that there are obstacles to action based on rational appeals. This is so because he believes that rational arguments tend to raise questions rather than to answer them. Emotional appeals, on the other hand, attempt to stimulate the individual to carry through impulses which he already has.

Advertisers, McGarry writes, have found that effective advertising contains a bit of rationality with a large dose of sentimentality. He states further that the fact that these appeals are effective indicates that "the average human mind is a montage of hasty impressions, fuzzy generalities, bromidic wall-motto sentiments, self-justifications and sentimentalities."[25]

McGarry cites a number of benefits which accrue to society as a result of advertising. Among those that he mentions are: (1) the standardization of wants through advertising is, in part, the basis for

---

[23]*Ibid.*, p. 133.

[24]McGarry doesn't define what he means by rational. However, this sentence seems to imply that a rational consumer is one whose choices are made after at least some deliberation, rather than for emotional reasons. McGarry does not present evidence indicating the validity of this paragraph.

[25]Quoted by McGarry in "The Propaganda Function in Marketing," p. 135, from Victor Schwab, "Ten Copy Appeals," *Printers' Ink* (December 17, 1943), p. 17. Neither McGarry nor Schwab offer evidence supporting the statements in this paragraph. For Schwab to be able to write about the "average human mind," he would have had to study a representative sample of minds and come up with a set of characteristics of these minds which were average, e.g., modal characteristics.

the economies of mass production and (2) competition among advertisers induces them to improve their products so that they can "bally-
hoo" these improvements in their advertisements.

McGarry does not make any value judgments with respect to advertising. He recognizes and accepts the view that its function is to
persuade, not to present a balanced judgment. The right to persuade
and be persuaded is, in his opinion, an essential freedom. McGarry
assumes that each of us has the mentality and the fortitude to choose
and to accept or reject what he hears or what he reads.

The Contactual Function. McGarry thinks of the contactual
function as falling within the main task of marketing. That main task
is to make the adjustment between what people desire and what it
is practicable for business to supply. Since this is the principal task,
he reasons, it follows that contacts must be made at each successive
step in the marketing process. McGarry labels as the contactual function "the searching out of the market for the purpose of finding out who
the potential customers or the potential sources are and then of making
and maintaining connections between those who have goods to offer and
those who want them.[26]

Through these contacts, McGarry believes, flow the information
which consumers need regarding the goods available and their sources
and the information which producers need concerning consumers and
their wants. The maintenance of contactual relationships forms the
framework for the structure of marketing which McGarry states is
necessary in any economy in which production is divorced from consumption.

The contactual function may be initiated by either the seller or
buyer. In general so long as goods are pressing on the market for
disposal, as is usual in the sale of manufactured products, sellers take
the initiative. McGarry believes that regardless of whether the seller
or the buyer takes the initiative, the essence of the contactual function
is the investigation of market potentials, the selection of the most suitable respondents (customers or sources), and the development of
mutual confidence and respect between the initiator and the respondents.

---

[26]McGarry uses the term "source" to mean the available or potential sellers of a
product. See Edmund D. McGarry, "The Contactual Function in Marketing," *The
Journal of Business* (April, 1951), p. 96. This statement of the contactual function
differs slightly from an earlier statement of the function presented by McGarry in
another source. See p. 90 of this study.

The contactual function is most effectively carried out on a person-to-person basis,[27] according to McGarry, because the contactual relationship between buyers and sellers is essentially a human relationship.[28] He believes that the result of the performance of the contactual function is the building of a structure for cooperative action.

In the case of buyers and sellers whose business transactions emphasize short-run considerations, such a structure is not likely to develop. However, McGarry believes that when buyers and sellers focus on the long-run welfare of their business, they are led to think in terms of a continuous business relationship. It then becomes apparent that each is dependent upon the other and that cooperation between them is to their mutual advantage.

Once the attitude of mutual interdependence emerges, McGarry writes, it becomes necessary that some agency assume the leadership in the cooperative effort. While the leadership is sometimes taken by large wholesalers or retailers, producers typically assume this role. This leadership, McGarry believes, acts to weld together the chain of contacts between the producer and the consumers. He believes that it is the function of the leader of such a chain not only to prevent friction between the various links and to keep them in balance but also to furnish the incentive and drive which will keep them operating effectively.[29]

McGarry further believes that as the chain of contacts between the producer and the consumer develops, it tends to become institutionalized, i.e., each agency tends to look upon itself less as an independent business unit and more as a part of a larger entity; and it becomes the interest of each agency to maintain the structure as a whole and thus provide continuously profitable business for all. "The chain of contacts," McGarry writes, "once it has become established, provides the mechanism for a continuous two-way line of communication between the producer and the consumer and a linkage of their interests."[30]

McGarry distinguishes between the structure of marketing and the contactual structure of marketing. In his view the former term refers to the network of trade channels through which the ownership flow moves. Since this concept, he states, leaves out of consideration

---

[27]The word effectively, as used in this sentence, apparently refers to the successful acquisition of sales.

[28]It is not clear whether this statement is intended to apply to the setting of potentials.

[29]McGarry's ideas seem to be intended to apply to consumer goods only. They would appear also to be substantially applicable to industrial marketing.

[30]Edmund D. McGarry, "The Contactual Function in Marketing," *The Journal of Business* (April, 1951), pp. 102–103.

the fact that many contacts are made and maintained without any transactions taking place between the parties, it is necessary to create a new concept known as the contactual structure of marketing. A contactual marketing structure may be either integrated or nonintegrated.

In the vertically integrated contactual structure, McGarry writes, all contacts lead to or from the owner enterprise, e.g., a chain store corporation. Such integrated institutions, he states, are seldom closed systems since some of the units of the system buy from agencies outside the system and other units sell to outside agencies.

As for the nonintegrated contactual structure, a manufacturer must maintain contacts with his sources of material and with his wholesalers, the wholesalers must maintain contact with their sources (manufacturers) and with their customers (retailers), and the retailers must maintain contact with their sources (wholesalers) and their customers (consumers). McGarry understands that it is usually necessary for a firm to maintain many contacts in addition to those which actually yield business. The maintenance of contacts which do not produce business may prove valuable if each of the parties obtains information necessary to operate his business intelligently. Essentially, McGarry thinks, a network of contactual relationships constitutes a device through which the goods that producers make and the goods that the consumers want are adjusted to each other or through which producers themselves are adjusted to consumers. He states that this adjustment takes place by means of selection from many alternatives.

McGarry writes that the contactual structure of marketing is both fluid and stable. It is fluid because any unit of the structure deals with its sources and customers on a transaction[31] basis, which is temporary and can change from one contact to another without notice and without embarrassment. In spite of this fluidity, McGarry believes that there is a stable aspect of any contactual marketing structure which stems from the mutual affinity that tends to grow up between two persons or enterprises and causes them to prefer to deal with each other rather than someone else.

Almost any well-established enterprise, McGarry states, can name dozens or hundreds of companies with which it has dealt for years or even generations. The marketing contacts of an enterprise at any given time, he deduces, are likely to vary in strength all the way from

---

[31]McGarry does not specify whether he intends the word "transaction" to refer to one or a small number of exchanges, or a long series of exchanges, or both. However, the point he is making here is that beyond any one transaction, regardless of whether it involves a few or many exchanges, there are usually no formal commitments to continue to carry on business.

those which are so firmly attached that they would not deal with a competitor unless powerful incentives were offered, through those which are completely indifferent as to whether they deal with this firm or some other, to those with such a negative attitude that they will deal elsewhere unless strong inducements are offered.

McGarry believes it is clear that the cost of dealing with continuous contacts is much less than that of dealing with casual contacts. This is so, he reasons, because in dealing with regular customers it can be assumed that the parties already know each other and neither party needs to investigate the other. Moreover, the transaction is more easily undertaken, and there is less inclination to haggle about terms. McGarry speculates that if an enterprise could confine its entire selling activities to regular and consistent customers, it might reduce its cost of marketing by 10 to 20 per cent.[32]

Established contactual relationships contribute to the making of sales, McGarry thinks, because they constitute one of many elements of product differentiation. This is so because the prospective buyer learns to know the seller and what he has to offer, and the seller becomes acquainted with the character of the buyer. They become adjusted to each other, McGarry writes, in such a way as to communicate their ideas with mutual understanding. The effect of this differentiation is that it allows the seller to increase his sales at a given price, maintain his sales at a higher price, or increase his sales at a higher price. Effective contactual relationships, McGarry believes, tend to move the demand curve for a seller's product upward and to the right. Effective contactual relationships initiated by a buyer are likely to move the supply curves for the products he buys downward and to the right.

McGarry has reason to believe that short-run profit maximizing is not the objective of many enterprises in the American economy. He assumes that the objective for many enterprises is permanence and stability[33] and concludes that, for this reason, the problem of developing and maintaining continuous contacts takes on a great deal of significance. In his view business cannot expect to shift its contacts from day to day and still attain the permanence of an institution. It is clear, he asserts, that few large modern businesses can exist wholly

---

[32]McGarry does not present any factual evidence to support the statements made in this paragraph.

[33]The profit objective implication of McGarry's assumption is that many enterprises seek neither short- or long-run profit maximization. Rather, they conduct their affairs so as to remain in business and earn what the owners regard as acceptable profits.

upon casual contacts entered into for immediate profit with no thought of future business.

McGarry's Functional Analysis: Methodology

McGarry's study of marketing functions is essentially speculative and deductive. As a long-time student of marketing, he has developed a mental image of marketing and how it operates.

McGarry's image is such that he thinks of marketing as a social mechanism that develops along with the growth of any economy in order to facilitate the adjustment of man and his environment. A marketing system designed to perform this social role is necessary, he deduces, because he assumes that people's wants, in so far as they apply to specific items of goods, are created by environmental factors and that goods cannot be made under conditions of mass production to meet all the varying specifications of individual consumers or users. If this is true, he reasons, "then it becomes a major task of marketing to reconcile the notions of potential users as to what they desire with the products that businessmen find it practical to provide."[34]

The performance of the contactual, propaganda, merchandising, pricing, physical distribution, and termination functions, McGarry reasons, is necessary for this adjustment to be effected. This is so, he asserts, because goods must be found or devised that will, as nearly as possible, meet the preconceived notions of users as to nature, quality, and price. Also, goods must be presented at the proper time and under the most favorable conditions to appeal to users. Potential consumers, moreover, must be conditioned to accept the goods as the best possible compromise between what they think they want and what they can get.

McGarry's image and discussion of the propaganda and contactual functions also appear to be based on a mixture of speculation, deduction, and limited induction. This statement can be illustrated with respect to the propaganda function as follows:

1. McGarry speculates that a substantial number of retail salesmen do not sell but merely facilitate the sale. He then deduces that, because of this circumstance, advertising has to take a substantial part of the responsibility for making sales.

2. McGarry speculates that consumers do not make rational choices and that they do not like to exert the effort to think rationally. He also speculates that effective advertising copy must be expressed in terms in which the consumer thinks. McGarry then deduces that

---

[34] McGarry, "Some Functions of Marketing Reconsidered," p. 278.

effective advertising copy should largely contain emotional appeals rather than rational arguments.

With respect to the contactual function, McGarry's methodology can be illustrated as follows:

1. McGarry's image of marketing is such that he regards that its main task is to make the adjustment between what people desire and what it is practical for business to supply. Since he regards this as marketing's principal task, he then deduces that contacts must be made at each successive step in the marketing process.
2. McGarry either speculates or deduces, or both, that the essence of the contactual function is the investigation of market potentials, the selection of the most suitable customers or sources, and the development of mutual confidence and respect between the initiator and the respondents.
3. McGarry deduces that when buyers and sellers are consciously concerned about the long-run welfare of their respective businesses, they think in terms of mutual interdependence and continuous business relationships. When these attitudes emerge, McGarry speculates that (a) it becomes necessary for some marketing agency to take the leadership in welding together the chain of contacts between producer and consumer and (b) chains of contacts between producer and consumer tend to become institutionalized.
4. McGarry deduces that the cost of dealing with continuous contacts is significantly less than that of dealing with casual contacts. This deduction is made by McGarry because he believes that buyers and sellers who deal with each other regularly (a) do not have to investigate each other and (b) are less inclined to haggle about terms.
5. McGarry speculates that established contactual relationships enable buyers and sellers to become adjusted to each other and to communicate their ideas with mutual understanding. He then deduces that the effect of this mutual adjustment is (a) a tendency for the demand curve for the seller's product to be shifted upward and to the right or (b) a tendency for the supply curves of the products purchased by the buyer to be shifted downward and to the right.
6. McGarry speculates that permanence and stability rather than short or long-run profit maximizing is the objective of many enterprises in the American economy. He then deduces that the development and maintenance of continuous contacts is highly important to many enterprises in order to achieve their objective of permanence and stability.

In general, McGarry's articles contain very little documentation. Where he makes assumptions, he makes this fact known explicitly. However, for the most part, important positive statements are made without reference to substantiating evidence.

Evaluation of McGarry's Functional Analysis

McGarry has apparently not completed his contribution to marketing theory since his theoretical publications have not yet dealt in detail with four of the six marketing functions he lists as necessary to the performance of the major task of a marketing system in a private enterprise economy. Presumably he will do this at a later date.

In developing his theory of marketing, McGarry wishes to explain marketing phenomena.[35] Initially such a theory, he states, represents conjecture and speculation. In his view a marketing theory needs to fit the facts and contribute to understanding and insight. Theories that meet these tests will, according to McGarry, constitute carefully reasoned and refined statements which will fit situations and aid in explaining what is happening in marketing.

McGarry makes no claim that his contributions are acceptable under these criteria. In fact he appears to recognize that they largely represent speculation and deductions from assumptions. He also recognizes the extent to which his contributions rest on observations and that the observations are not such as to permit generalization.

In the absence of supporting evidence, McGarry's contributions might be evaluated in terms of credibility, consistency, and comparison with the views of other marketing students. Since a substantial part of McGarry's contribution rests on conclusions logically deduced from assumptions, it is appropriate to question whether the assumptions are correct and whether an understanding of reality necessarily is obtained from logical deductions based on even correct assumptions.[36]

An example of an assumption made by McGarry, which in this writer's view is questionable, is the following:

> The ideal to which marketing aspires is to distribute to consumers all the goods that full employment of all resources makes possible in such a way that each can secure what he wants within his income, with a minimum of delay and inconvenience.[37]

---

[35]McGarry does not explicitly define what he means by the term explain. However, judging from his analysis of marketing functions, McGarry is attempting to explain marketing phenomena by developing accurate understanding of (a) the role of marketing in an economy and (b) the nature and effective execution of specific marketing functions.

[36]Professor Reavis Cox, for one, in his course on Theory in Marketing, has questioned whether reality is necessarily ascertained by making logical deductions from even accurate assumptions.

[37]McGarry, "Some Functions of Marketing Reconsidered," published in Cox and Alderson (eds.), *Theory in Marketing*, p. 268. In this statement McGarry personifies marketing. He does not specify who it is that has ideals.

This kind of statement appears to emanate from wishful thinking on McGarry's part. In this writer's opinion it is questionable whether any group of marketing practitioners seeks to conduct itself in accordance with this objective. It is, moreover, doubtful that federal, state, and local governments regulate marketing on the basis of this goal.

McGarry's assumption that the social task of marketing is to make the adjustment between what people desire and what it is practical for business to supply appears to be more plausible. This assumption seems to be consistent, for example, with the belief held by three other long-time marketing students, R. S. Vaile, E. T. Grether, and Reavis Cox, who state that the basic tasks of marketing are (1) to direct the use of resources and allocate scarce supplies in conformity with existing demand and (2) to aid in making consumption dynamic in conformity with changes in an economy's ability to cater to human wants.

Part of McGarry's explanation of marketing propaganda, i.e., advertising, is in agreement with views held by a number of other marketing analysts. In this category would fall his acceptance of the fact that advertising is intended to persuade and not to present a balanced judgment. Also, when he views advertising as inducing product improvement and making possible, in part, the economies of mass production through standardization of wants, McGarry seems to hold a modal view.

However, McGarry's belief that the consumer buyer is imperfectly rational and that he hates the labor of rational thinking runs counter to the view held by other analysts, notably Wroe Alderson. Alderson believes that perhaps two thirds of the consumer buyers in the United States are rational problem solvers whose activities are largely similar to those of industrial purchasing agents.[38] Also, McGarry feels that advertising messages are likely to be more productive of sales if they emphasize emotional appeals, while Alderson holds the view that the consumer should be approached primarily as a problem solver who must first be convinced that he has a problem and then that the product offered will facilitate a solution.[39]

---

[38]Wroe Alderson, *Marketing Behavior and Executive Action* (Homewood, Illinois: Richard D. Irwin, Inc., 1957), pp. 179–181.

[39]The question may be raised as to whether a consumer might not use rational means to satisfy an emotional need. Alderson's view of the consumer does not appear to exclude such behavior. However, Mc Garry's position implies that impulse rather than deliberation, i.e., a weighing of facts, plays an important part in the making of consumer choices.

Neither McGarry nor Alderson presents evidence to support his respective position, so it is not possible to come to any conclusions as to the accuracy of their views. Alderson, too, is a long-time student of marketing, and the fact that his position differs so markedly from that of McGarry raises at least some doubt as to the accuracy of McGarry's views with respect to consumer behavior and the substance of effective advertising copy.

McGarry believes that the human mind is a montage of impressions, fuzzy generalities, bromidic wall-motto sentiments, self-justification and sentimentalities. He, moreover, assumes that with respect to advertising each consumer has the mentality and the fortitude to choose and to accept or reject what he hears or what he reads. While McGarry is no doubt correct that a fuzzy mind can choose, it probably makes choice decisions on the basis of fuzzy reasons; and it is difficult to believe that such a mind will choose wisely.

While McGarry's discussion of the contactual function lacks documentation, much of it appears plausible. Viewed in its entirety, however, his discussion appears to be more an ideal picture of the performance of the contactual function than an explanation of reality. This writer does not doubt that if the contactual function were, in fact, performed in the manner described by McGarry, society and business enterprises would benefit. However, if a theoretical contribution must, as McGarry states, "fit the facts," this writer hesitates to accept his description of the contactual function because it appears unlikely that a large fraction of marketing practitioners performs the contactual function in the manner set forth by McGarry and that its performance works out as perfectly as he views it.

Since McGarry's several contributions to date lack supporting evidence, this writer is inclined to view what he has written as largely representing his personal opinion and belief. As such, they deserve no more credibility than the opinions of other long-time students of marketing whose opinions may or may not agree with those held by McGarry. Perhaps, at a later date, empirical research by McGarry or other students of marketing will offer a basis for judging the extent to which McGarry's contribution "fits the facts" as they pertain to marketing functions.

Chapter 7

ORGANIZED BEHAVIOR SYSTEMS AND THE THEORY OF MARKET BEHAVIOR

Wroe Alderson's *Marketing Behavior and Executive Action* (1957) represented a significant contribution to marketing literature.[1] In this book Alderson, a long-time student of and participant in marketing, appears to have set down many of his ideas relevant to the practice and understanding of marketing. During his career Alderson has had experience as a marketing consultant, government official, and university professor.

Alderson's Concept of Science and Theory

Alderson defines a science as the orderly investigation of some class of natural phenomena. It consists of laws, generalizations, principles, and theory and the descriptive facts and results of "crucial experiments" on which these are based.[2] He agrees with those philosophers of science who believe that the most important goal of science is increasing the empirical accuracy of "laws or principles."

Science, Alderson writes, should seek to improve its answers to important questions. With respect to the field of marketing, important questions, in his opinion, are those which bear on our knowledge of marketing phenomena or relate to the efficient use of resources in pursuing marketing objectives.[3] Desirable goals for marketing scientists

---

[1] The bulk of this chapter is based on this volume.

[2] Alderson does not set forth his concepts of law, generalization, or principle. His concept of theory is presented below. The phrase "crucial experiment" is not defined. One dictionary of philosophical terms defines "crucial experiment" as follows: "an experiment so arranged that its results will be final or crucial in solving a problem: as the introduction of a flame into a jar to determine whether one of a group of inflammable gases is present or not." See James M. Baldwin (ed.), *Dictionary of Philosophy and Psychology* (New York: Peter Smith, 1940), Vol. 1, p. 362.

[3] Alderson apparently takes this view from C. West Churchman's pragmatic ideas of science. See C. West Churchman, "Basic Research in Marketing," published in Reavis Cox and Wroe Alderson (eds.), *Theory in Marketing* (Homewood, Illinois: Richard D. Irwin, Inc., 1950), pp. 4–7.

consist of (1) explaining why things work out as they do in marketing, (2) the discovery of empirical regularities or functional relationships that permit prediction,[4] and (3) setting forth the bases for controlling the course of marketing events.

In Alderson's view marketing theorists should labor toward the goal of creating a general theory of marketing. Such a theory should be composed of a set of propositions which are consistent among themselves and are relevant to the actual practice of marketing. These propositions, preferably in the form of mathematical statements, should be empirically testable hypotheses. Marketing theory, according to Alderson, should be based on marketing facts if it is to have practical value; but the accumulation of marketing facts without a guiding theoretical structure is an uncertain foundation for an advancing knowledge and mastery of a field.

While Alderson is of the opinion that marketing theorists should aim to develop marketing theory in accordance with this view, it is his opinion that it is too early to expect such a result. An adequate theory of marketing at the present stage, Alderson writes, is likely to be in the nature of nonmathematical, vague, general statements, perhaps even sweeping statements, about marketing. Such marketing theory would be acceptable to Alderson if it provides perspective[5] for marketing executives and students being trained for marketing occupations. This conclusion apparently stems from Alderson's broad marketing experience. In his view marketing executives need such a general theoretical perspective as an aid in solving their problems.[6] He further writes that the effective training of future marketing practitioners requires perspective about marketing in addition to knowledge about its institutions and processes.

Alderson sums up his thoughts on the nature and objectives of early versions of marketing theory as follows:

> Adequate theoretical perspective should aid the student and the market analyst in understanding . . . differences among substantially, but not precisely, similar, marketing situations . . . and in making corresponding decisions about the course of action to be followed in

---

[4]Alderson states that functional relationships permit prediction in terms of specified assumptions.

[5]This writer's dictionary defines perspective as meaning a far-reaching mental view in which things appear in proper relation to each other.

[6]In Alderson's view a marketing executive is said to have a problem when he is uncertain as to a future course of action.

each case. Marketing theory under this conception is definitely relevant to marketing practice. In some instances it can be an immediate guide to action. In many more cases it can give direction to the research effort needed to develop the facts on which to base a course of action. In the longer view, theory should facilitate the accumulation and integration of a body of knowledge,[7] so that what is learned through coping with one set of problems can be brought to bear on others.[8]

Alderson is of the opinion that the work of marketing theorists is never-ending. If they work to improve the accuracy of their answers to important marketing questions, new facts are likely to be uncovered which suggest new generalizations or revisions in the body of theory; and new developments in theory, he writes, will lead to new areas of investigation or types of experiment. The continuing development of marketing science, Alderson writes, will aid marketing practitioners through the discovery of principles of action and the development of scientific techniques for the orderly investigation and solution of concrete marketing problems.

The Functionalist Approach to Marketing Theory

In Alderson's opinion marketing theory should be a component part of a general science of human behavior. This position stems from his concept of marketing which holds that marketing is the exchange taking place between consuming groups on the one hand and supplying groups on the other.[9] Moreover, it has been Alderson's experience that (1) marketing executives are very much aware that they are dealing with people and (2) it is essential for the market analyst to formulate most of his problem in terms of group behavior.

---

[7]Alderson writes that a minimum requirement in the construction of marketing science is the development of an organized conceptual framework for ordering and interpreting its factual content.

[8]Wroe Alderson, *Marketing Behavior and Executive Action* (Homewood, Illinois: Richard D. Irwin, Inc., 1957), p. 7.

[9]Alderson's concept of marketing has many dimensions as is evidenced by the following quotations which appear in various parts of *Marketing Behavior and Executive Action:*
   a. Marketing is oriented to action.
   b. Every phase of marketing can be understood as human behavior within the framework of some operating system.
   c. All marketing activity is an aspect of the interaction among organized behavior systems related to each other in an ecological network.
   d. Perhaps the most essential function of a marketing firm is that of handling information and acting as a kind of switchboard connecting the consumer who has a specialized need with the specialized product which can satisfy his need.

Alderson terms his approach the functionalist approach to marketing theory. He writes:

> Functionalism is that approach to science which begins by identifying some system of action and then tries to determine how and why it works as it does. Functionalism stresses the whole system and undertakes to interpret the parts in terms of how they serve the system. Some writers who are actually advocates of functionalism prefer to speak of the holistic approach because of emphasis on the system as a whole. Functionalism generally recognizes that the operation of a system is likely to change over time and that the essence of science is its dynamic aspect. . . .

> The functionalist may . . . need to be cautioned to give adequate attention to structure. Actually, a sound functionalism in the social sciences concerns itself with the structure of operating systems. Both function and structure are embraced in the subject matter of scientific study; but the functionalist believes that function basically determines structure . . . rather than the reverse. . . . [The functionalist] . . . does not feel that he understands [a] situation if he goes no further than to describe the existing structure. He is impelled to find out what functions it is performing and, even more fundamentally how the group will have to function in order to survive.[10]

In Alderson's view there is a normative aspect to functionalism. "It is scarcely possible to give a correct interpretation of a group," he writes, "unless the student begins with a recognition and understanding of its actual or potential functions."[11] Alderson states that the functionalist is behaving as a scientist ". . . if the norms he applies are inherent in the systems he is studying and not imposed from without."[12] According to Alderson, ". . . the majority of systems seem to operate as if they were trying to survive, to grow, and to produce some kind of surplus or output. When the scientist observes pathological

---

e. Marketing starts with attempts to organize the market or to establish the processes of orderly marketing.
f. Marketing emphasizes the unique characteristic of individual need and the objective of achieving the most suitable assortments within the limitations of the goods available.
g. The goal of marketing is the matching of segments of supply and demand.
h. The version of marketing theory which is presented here may be regarded as an aspect of the general science of human behavior. It is related to economics, since it is concerned with the efficient correlation of means and ends. It is more allied to the broader social sciences in its conception of the social setting within which the individual or the operating group seeks to achieve their ends.

[10]Alderson, *Marketing Behavior and Executive Action*, pp. 16–17.

[11]*Ibid.*, p. 17.

[12]*Ibid.*, p. 17.

behavior in some system, he is judging it to be abnormal in terms of his conception of how a healthy system operates."[13]

Functionalism is interested in theory, Alderson writes, as a conceptual tool which will assist in dealing with factual data and with problems of action. The functionalist approach studies both the structure and functions of systems. Emphasis, however, is placed on function because the functionalist believes that function basically determines structure in group behavior, rather than the reverse.

Alderson asserts that functionalism is the most promising approach for theoretical development in marketing because it begins with concepts which can be applied to all types of commodities and all types of firms which participate in marketing. Functionalist analysts identify the functions of marketing and then show how these apply in one situation after another. According to Alderson any comprehensive list of marketing functions, to be useful, must have relevance to the groups of organized behavior systems engaged in marketing. He further writes that functional analysis can be used either as interpretation or in the solution of marketing problems. The emphasis of the functionalist approach on how things work and what needs to be done in order to make them work better makes it particularly useful in marketing because the study of marketing is primarily concerned with the solution of practical problems.

As for methodology, Alderson states, the functionalist uses a combination of empirical research techniques and deductive reasoning. Functionalism is, moreover, eclectic because it accepts whatever useful findings are unearthed in other sciences.

Among the social sciences, Alderson writes, sociology, psychology, and anthropology have contributed most to the development of a general science of human behavior. Of these he has concluded that sociology is the most useful for his purposes because it is concerned with the normal functioning of groups, with the basic element making for group coherence, and with the satisfactions which groups produce for their members.

According to Alderson the ultimate objective of the functionalist approach is to understand how marketing firms and households attempt to solve their marketing problems and to discover principles by which they might do it better. The macromarketing objective of the functionalist is to understand how an entire marketing system continues to evolve through the activities of its components.

---

[13]*Ibid.*, pp. 17–18.

Organized Behavior Systems

Alderson states that the functionalist approach to marketing theory begins with the study of organized behavior systems because the functions of marketing are performed by such systems or by individuals acting within such systems. In this connection Alderson emphatically asserts:

> A marketing executive or market analyst is not equipped to solve marketing problems unless he can think in organizational terms. Marketing plans which are conceived only in terms of money, goods, and their physical movement are doomed to fail. A marketing plan must be executed through sales organizations, distribution channels, and other organized behavior systems. . . .[14]

Alderson conceives of an organized behavior system as one which coordinates the activities of a group or groups of human beings in an established pattern of behavior. The system, he states, may be regarded as including the instruments and resources utilized in its operations. In his view these instruments are not part of the group which consists only of the human beings present in the system. The instruments, however, belong to the system in the sense of being within its possession and control. The functionalist's interest in such systems is to study (1) the formation and persistence of groups, (2) the structure of groups, and (3) the internal and external adjustments of groups to meet changing conditions.

A behavior system may be termed an operating system, Alderson states, when it involves inputs and outputs. He does not, however, explicitly define marketing inputs and outputs.[15] In discussing the output of marketing Alderson emphasizes that progressive differentiation of products and services is extremely important in defining the values created by marketing. In taking this view he states that he is assuming that each individual's need is different from every other individual's need in one or more respects. On the basis of this assumption he states that the basic economic process is the gradual differentiation of goods up to the point at which they pass into the hands of consumers.

---

[14]*Ibid.*, p. 47.

[15]The inputs of an operating system may be conceived to consist of the factors of production in physical terms. The basic agents could be grouped under such headings as capital, space used, equipment used, selling personnel, nonselling personnel, advertising, display, etc. The outputs of such a system could be regarded as including services such as delivery, credit, range of choice, quality of advice given by the marketing practitioner, and the relation between the quality and prices of the goods offered.

Refrigerators or packages of corn flakes, Alderson writes, may all look alike as they come off the production line in the factory. However, such products are then differentiated when they are shipped to various parts of the country. In Alderson's view every step along the way results in shaping materials more and more precisely to fit the needs of specific consumers.

Alderson states that one of the characteristics of operating systems is division of labor which he defines as the assignment of operating functions to individuals or subgroups within the larger group. He writes that division of labor can take place along several different lines: division by stages of the process, division by segments of output, and division by type of input. Division of labor by stages of the process involves successive levels in distribution channels. As an example of division of labor by segments of output, Alderson cites the case of a large company selling both coffee and breakfast cereal which uses separate salesmen on each. Division of labor by type of input, according to Alderson, means that there are various specialists engaged in such activities as physical handling, selling, and advertising.

In discussing the structure of operating systems, Alderson states that there are many possible variations in the design of a system as a whole and that the range of variation consists of a few structural elements. Each of these elements, he asserts, must be considered by the organization analyst or the marketing executive in creating or improving an operating system.

The elements of structure listed by Alderson are seriality, parallelism, and circularity. He defines seriality as the state of being arranged in a sequence of steps and stages, with the process under consideration flowing from one stage to another. Parallelism refers to a situation in which the same general type of product moves to market through several separate channels starting with separate segments of supply, serving different segments of demand, and not showing up in the same intermediary establishment anywhere along the way. Alderson writes that circularity refers to a sequence of steps arranged in such a way that the process finally returns to the point from which it started. He states that the principal application of circularity in marketing is to the movement of information rather than to the movement of goods. In an operating system, he writes, information flows out from the central command to bring about appropriate action within the organization. Circularity is achieved when information flows back that the action has succeeded or has been a complete or partial failure.

Alderson's discussion of the structure of an operating system includes what he calls the structural postulate of marketing. Effective management of any input-output system, Alderson writes, requires that the largest proportion of the system's operations be routinized. This is so, Alderson writes, because more business can be transacted in routine fashion with a given amount of effort than when all of the terms and conditions have to be negotiated. He defines routine activities as those which can be repeated time after time with no essential change in form. Strategic actions, Alderson states, are those which pertain to nonrecurring situations. He writes that these actions are strategic because they may affect a whole subsequent sequence of activities and because they may involve substantial uncertainties as to the future outlook of the company. Alderson distinguishes between a strategic transaction and one that is routine when he states that the former is a fully negotiated transaction while in the latter many of the terms have already been established by previous negotiations.[16]

Alderson writes that most operating systems have at least one decision center for coordinating the activities of the system. In many small firms the power of decision is held by the owner. However, large operating systems require multiple decision centers because too many things must be decided for all of them to be referred to a single center. In the latter type of situation Alderson states that there is necessarily some type of structural arrangement connecting the decision centers.

Alderson concludes his discussion of organized behavior systems by discussing abnormal behavior in such systems. Alderson writes that abnormal behavior in organized behavior systems can result from:

1. The tendency to substitute ideology for information.
2. Excessive expectations within the organization.
3. Existence of a self-dramatizing leader.
4. A strong drive for power among important individuals in the organization.
5. Existence of internal conflict.
6. Existence of a top heavy structure.
7. A situation in which an operating group as a whole acquires a psychological fixation in which it either underestimates or exaggerates the capacity of the system.

---

[16]This is not quite accurate. A strategic transaction may or may not be fully negotiated.

The Theory of Market Behavior

In his theory of market behavior Alderson states that consumer demand in the United States is radically heterogeneous, i.e., consumer tastes and requirements are highly diverse. This heterogeneity of demand, he writes, is independent of the actions of sellers. The household is the unit which consumes goods and services, and for most households the purchasing agent is the wife. Moreover, the housewife, as a buyer, is a rational problem-solver who attempts to assemble an assortment of goods which will meet the anticipated needs of the household. In spending her income she tends to allocate it so that the utility derived from the last dollar spent on each product is equal.[17]

Alderson believes that marketing practitioners formulate their policies so as to cater to this heterogeneous demand. That is, they strive to develop their market offerings, e.g., product, location, service, package, price, etc., in such a way so as to appeal to consumer needs better than competitors do. This is competition for differential advantage, a concept first developed by J. M. Clark and later further developed by E. H. Chamberlain. This type of competition leads to heterogeneity of supply according to Alderson.

Given heterogeneity in demand and supply, a matching process is necessary in order to meet the needs of consumers. Marketing middlemen effect the matching of heterogeneous segments of supply with heterogeneous segments of demand.[18] This matching is accomplished through various types of sorting: sorting-out, accumulation, allocation, and assorting.

Alderson defines sorting-out as a process in which a collection is broken into various types of goods. This process, he states, results in a set of separate supplies which can be regarded as homogeneous in terms of the classification being used by the sorter.[19] Accumulation is a process in which small homogeneous supplies are added together to create larger supplies. This accumulation may involve the building up of a larger supply over a period of time, or it may represent the bringing together in a single place products which meet standard specifications but are drawn from different localities.[20]

---

[17]Alderson, *Marketing Behavior and Executive Action*, pp. 232–33. This statement is questioned on p. 112.

[18]Alderson seems to be excluding the matching performed by producers.

[19]Alderson points out that some of this is done by processors.

[20]Alderson points out that these processes serve several purposes, e.g., promotes the ease of transportation, facilitates proper utilization of space, and provides a continuous flow of suitable materials for large processing and manufacturing operations.

Alderson refers to two types of allocation. These are internal and external allocation, and both mean the breaking down of a homogeneous supply into smaller quantities determined by the requirements of each use situation. In internal allocation there may be two or more possible uses; and each unit of supply, according to Alderson, is assigned to the most productive use until productivity is equal at the margin, i.e., the marginal productivity principle. External allocation, according to Alderson, is guided by the marginal revenue principle. Alderson writes that if a company has several sales territories, it will distribute its products among these territories so as to obtain the same revenue from the last unit sold in each territory. Moreover, under the marginal revenue principle, a seller will be encouraged to expand his sales in all directions until the last unit sold produces a revenue which barely covers all the costs of production and selling. Assorting is the putting together of unlike supplies in accordance with some pattern determined by demand.

Marketing middlemen are specialists in these sorting operations and contribute to lowering the costs of marketing by performing the matching process more efficiently than could producers or consumers.[21] Marketing efficiency is also enhanced through the routinizing of transactions by such devices as a one-price policy, credit investigation, self-service, and packaging.

Marketing middlemen, in addition to making marketing more efficient, are, together with producers, engaged in the exploitation of joint opportunity. That is, combined in a channel system, they have mutual interests in the sale of a product. In addition to increasing sales and profits through differential advantage, buyers or suppliers can contribute to the attainment of this objective for themselves by securing the cooperation of other channel components in the execution of their marketing plans. The technique through which this cooperation is secured is negotiation. A barrier to the integration of marketing channels, Alderson writes, is the discrepancy of assortments.[22] Alderson illustrates the nature of this barrier by citing the example of a

---

[21]Specialization, of course, permits individuals and enterprises to use to best advantage any particular differences in skill and resources. The result of specialization is usually lower costs and/or larger output.

[22]Alderson explains that discrepancy of assortments exists because the most convenient or constructive association of goods changes at each stage in the flow of merchandise from producer to consumer.

retail grocer who typically relies on different wholesale sources for meat, produce, and packaged groceries. The requirements for storage, handling, and other aspects of the wholesale function are quite different in these three product fields. If it were not for the discrepancy of assortments, Alderson avers, marketing channels might be more frequently integrated from top to bottom.

In presenting his insights on selling tools, Alderson emphasizes the importance of advertising and personal selling for obtaining sales. He writes that advertising will produce sales if it recognizes that the consumer is a rational problem-solver and if it informs and persuades the consumer that particular needs are important and that specific products and brands will satisfy consumer needs. According to Alderson competition is the dynamic catalyst of the marketing system, producing *inter alia*, product changes, price changes, changes in marketing institutions, and channel arrangements.

Organized Behavior Systems and the Theory of Market Behavior: Evaluation

Alderson makes no grandiose claims for his concept of an organized behavior system and his theory of market behavior. Rather, they are intended to give the marketing executive and student perspective which will aid in understanding marketing and in solving marketing problems. Individuals concerned with marketing, Alderson states, need to know more about marketing than its institutions and the activities of individuals engaged in marketing.

The development of perspective is not regarded by Alderson as the final product of science. Rather, he regards the marketing perspective which constitutes his contribution merely as an initial step in the direction of marketing science. His ultimate objective with respect to the development of marketing science is the discovery of principles of action for marketing practitioners and the development of scientific techniques for the orderly investigation and solution of concrete marketing problems.

Alderson's argument that it is important for marketing executives and market analysts to understand the operation and utility of organized behavior systems appears convincing. His point that the successful execution of a marketing plan frequently depends on the proper organization and operation of such units as sales organizations and distribution channels is self-evident. It is not self-evident, however, that such units are organized behavior systems or that marketing effectiveness is, in fact, enhanced by treating them as organized behavior systems.

The concept of the nature of an organized behavior system appears plausible and contributes to the student's and executive's understanding of such organizations. Moreover, his discussion of the structural features of abnormal behavior in such systems would appear to be useful to marketing executives concerned with the formation and successful operation of marketing organizations.

Much of the portrait of marketing presented by Alderson in his theory of market behavior appears to be in accord with that contained in marketing literature, e.g., heterogeneity of consumer demand, competition for differential advantage, sorting efficiency of marketing middlemen, and the role of intrachannel cooperation. However, several aspects of his theory, on the basis of available knowledge, appear questionable.

Alderson's statement[23] that consumer buyers allocate their expenditures in accordance with the marginal utility theory of consumer behavior appears to constitute acceptance of a view from economic theory which is only in the nature of conjecture and hypothesis. In writing about the marginal utility theory of consumer behavior, one economist, Raymond T. Bye, does not hold that consumers spend their money in this manner. Rather, he states that the marginal utility theory of consumer demand "shows how human beings would spend if they were completely rational, and if they had the time and capacity to make the necessary calculations; but the very statement of these 'ifs' shows the impossibility of the assumed conditions."[24]

Alderson's concept of internal and external allocation gives the impression that businessmen do in fact employ the principles of

---

[23]This statement appears to be a conclusion rather than an assumption. This view stems from the following quotation from Alderson:

   The application of the marginal principle takes place in a parallel way on the two sides of the market. There is a difference in terminology and in detailed application. As it applies to decisions by the buyer, marginality is expressed in the concept of marginal utility. The seller, on the other hand, is motivated by considerations of marginal productivity in creating goods for the market and by considerations of marginal revenue in allocating his output to various buyers in the market. The rational basis of allocation is identical for all of these situations. *Thus, market values as expressed in prices can truly be said to rest on a consensus of many judgments expressed through the process of dual allocation.* See Alderson, *Marketing Behavior and Executive Action*, pp. 232–33.

[24]R. T. Bye, *Principles of Economics* (5th ed.; New York: Appleton-Century-Crofts, Inc., 1956), p. 331.

marginal productivity and marginal revenue. While there is no question that the use of these principles would be economically rational, the extent to which businessmen do apply these principles is not known. In the case of the marginal revenue principle, it has been questioned whether businessmen are able to obtain the information necessary to apply this principle.[25]

In dealing with the question of consumer buying behavior, Alderson appears to take only cursory notice of the work of sociologists and social psychologists in this area. Their work up to now (e.g., influence of small groups on buyers' attitudes and behavior and the significance of a buyer's social class in determining his purchasing behavior) while not conclusive seems deserving of more extensive inclusion in any discussion of consumer behavior.[26]

Alderson attributes changes in marketing institutions to the striving by individual channel components to coordinate the channel in their respective interests. It appears that such an explanation should also state that new marketing institutions also arise in response to opportunities for market segmentation and the demand for more efficient performance of marketing tasks, e.g., discount houses, cash and carry wholesalers, and self-service supermarkets.

Alderson states that since, in his view, the consumer is a rational problem-solver, advertising copy which regards the consumer as a creature of habit, or as having emotions which influence her buying decisions, is relatively less effective in producing sales than advertising which informs and persuades the consumer buyer of the importance of certain needs and the efficacy of certain products and brands in satisfying needs.[27] Alderson may be correct in this view, but in the absence of supporting data one cannot, of course, determine the accuracy of the statement.

On the whole, Alderson's concept of an organized behavior system and his theory of market behavior represent a significant contribution to marketing theory. While this contribution, to a large extent, con-

---

[25]See Richard Lester, "Shortcomings of Marginal Analysis for Wage-Employment Problems," *American Economic Review* (March, 1946), pp. 77–78; See also Alfred R. Oxenfeldt, *Industrial Pricing and Market Prices* (New York: Prentice-Hall, Inc., 1951), Chapters 3 and 4.

[26]See, for example, David Riesman, *The Lonely Crowd*, in collaboration with Reuel Denny and Nathan Glazer (New Haven: Yale University Press, 1950); Muzafer Sherif and Carolyn W. Sherif, *An Outline of Social Psychology* (New York: Harper & Brothers, 1956); and W. Lloyd Warner, M. Meeker, and K. Eells, *Social Class in America* (Chicago: Science Research Associates, Inc., 1949).

[27]Alderson, *Marketing Behavior and Executive Action*, p. 278.

sists of an assembly of insights and hypotheses, these are clearly worthy of investigation in view of Alderson's rich experience in marketing.[28]

---

[28]Alderson lists the kind of research studies which might be undertaken so as to test the hypotheses which emanate from his concept of organized behavior systems and his theory of market behavior. See Wroe Alderson, "Areas for Basic Research in Marketing" (Mimeographed paper, Philadelphia, September 17, 1957). This paper may be obtained from Alderson Associates, Inc., 3 Penn Center Plaza, Philadelphia, Pennsylvania.

Chapter 8

ANALYSIS OF THE EFFICIENCY OF
MARKETING CHANNELS

Among the major contributions to marketing literature which have appeared in recent years, two have focused on developing techniques of analysis designed to aid in improving the efficiency of the work performed by marketing channels. Professors Reavis Cox and Charles S. Goodman have concentrated on developing tools for measuring and studying the magnitude and effectiveness of such work, and Professor Ralph Breyer has put forth what he calls a systemic approach to marketing which emphasizes the opportunity and need for analyzing and controlling the operations of groups of related distribution channels in much the same manner as the operations of individual marketing enterprises are analyzed and controlled.

Cox and Goodman Study: Channels and Flows in the Marketing of Housebuilding Materials

The study conducted by Professors Cox and Goodman was undertaken for the United States Housing and Home Finance Agency.[1] Originally these researchers had hoped that their inquiry could point up specific savings that could be effected in the marketing of the materials that went into the construction of homes. However, the information necessary for such an analysis was not available, and Professors Cox and Goodman were compelled to concentrate on (1) developing the analytical tools necessary for such an evaluation of the efficiency of the marketing of housebuilding materials and (2) collecting the information called for by these tools.

---

[1]Reavis Cox and Charles S. Goodman, *Channels and Flows in the Marketing of House-Building Materials* (3 vols.; Philadelphia: Mimeographed and published by the authors, 1954). See also Reavis Cox and Charles S. Goodman, "Marketing of Housebuilding Materials," *Journal of Marketing*, national quarterly publication of the American Marketing Association, Vol. XXI (July, 1956), pp. 36–61.

The kind of study which Professors Cox and Goodman found it practicable to undertake sought to answer the following questions with respect to a specific type of house, i.e., an "example house":[2]

1. How much marketing is performed in assembling the materials for building the example house?
2. How effective is the marketing of building materials?
3. How would common proposals for change affect the effectiveness of the marketing of house-building materials?[3]

Measurement of the Amount of Marketing Performed. The bulk of the effort that went into the Cox and Goodman study focused on answering the first of these three questions. In seeking this answer Professors Cox and Goodman decided that the requirements of their study dictated that the work performed in the marketing of house-building materials needed to be measured in real rather than in monetary terms.

This decision was based on their judgment that monetary measurement of this work would not be sufficiently informative for the purpose of obtaining satisfactory answers to the three basic questions posed by their inquiry. Moreover, Professors Cox and Goodman pointed out that managerial controls must frequently be imposed in real terms rather than in monetary ones, e.g., control over the number of salesmen employed, the distances they travel, and the number of calls they make.

Having come to this conclusion, Professors Cox and Goodman proceeded to develop seven measures which were intended to indicate the amount of marketing work performed in carrying building materials through marketing channels from points of extraction to the ultimate building site.[4] These measures stem from a concept of marketing which holds that the tasks assigned to marketing in our economy take the form of organizing and regulating a number of different but related flows. Professors Cox and Goodman explain that the marketing work done in each flow is measured by defining and counting one or more units of movement.

---

[2]Professors Cox and Goodman conducted their study in terms of a specific example house because (1) the funds at their disposal prevented their carrying out a broader study and (2) by concentrating on one type of house, they were able to research and analyze deeply rather than superficially.

[3]Cox and Goodman, *Channels and Flows in the Marketing of House-Building Materials*, Vol. III, p. 5.

[4]Professors Cox and Goodman emphasize the importance of analyzing the complete channel, i.e., from points of extraction to points of use or consumption, when evaluating the efficiency of marketing channels. They say that to conceive marketing in conventional terms as commencing when a product has been manufactured would prevent meaningful comparisons between alternatives and present a distorted view of the marketing work that must be performed to provide products for users or consumers.

The measures used were as follows:

1. The number of days required to produce and assemble at the building site each of the principle materials embodied in a house.

Professors Cox and Goodman regarded this measure as a crude indicator of the aggregate dimensions of the production and marketing task.

2. The dollar-days of investment accumulated in the materials embodied in a house as these goods moved down the channel from first extraction to final assembly at the site. (Professors Cox and Goodman defined a dollar-day of investment as the owning of one dollar's worth of a product or material for one day.)

This measure was intended to indicate the magnitude of the costs arising from the expenses of investment, storage, and risk. Professors Cox and Goodman state that this measure was also designed to permit some evaluation of whether the total time involved in getting specific materials to the building site was too high and some evaluation of the extent to which storage was concentrated at points where accumulated values were lowest.

3. The number of geographical places in which each building material was processed or handled.
4. The number of times the materials of a house are loaded, moved, and unloaded during their progress from the places at which they are extracted to the building site.
5. The number of ton-miles of transportation performed for these materials in their progress from places of extraction to the building site.

Professors Cox and Goodman write that measures 3, 4, and 5 were designed to permit an evaluation as to whether excessive amounts of movement were performed, whether an excessive number of sources were drawn upon for materials, the extent to which cross-hauling and back-hauling existed, and whether transportation was performed at those stages of processing when the work required would be at a minimum.

6. The number of owning and nonowning business entities that participate in the extracting, processing, and handling of building materials in their progress from places of extraction to the building site.
7. The number of transactions arranged in moving the materials from places of extraction to the building site. (Professors Cox and Goodman define a transaction as a transfer of the ownership of a product from one business entity to another. Transfers of ownership between independent business units and those between affiliated units were both counted as transactions.)

Measures 6 and 7 were intended to give some indication of the work performed in bringing together the business entities involved in marketing not only in the sense of an actual flow of orders but also in the development of relationships that may become routinized once they have been established.

Tools of Analysis.   In addition to developing the foregoing measures, Professors Cox and Goodman utilized two principal analytical devices to present what they term a complete channel analysis — the flow chart and the product monograph.[5]

The flow chart, an illustration of which is presented in Figure 9, shows the flow of a building material from the point of extraction to the building site of the example house.   This chart identifies the places where each physical object that eventually became the house originated and the business entities that owned and controlled the goods at these points.

The product monographs were designed to supplement the flow charts and consisted essentially of the following:

1. A detailed description of the product studied.
2. A detailed description of the marketing channel selected for analysis.
3. A description of variants in the marketing channels and their significance.
4. A list of omitted antecedents; the monograph presents conclusions as to their relative importance for the purposes of the study.
5. Opinions as to whether the channel analyzed contained any weakness that tended substantially to increase the marketing work performed over what would be required by more effectively organized channels.

The flow chart thus depicts the marketing work performed for each building material studied, and the product monograph analyzes the chart with a view to presenting conclusions as to the efficiency of this work.

In addition to these charts and monographs, Professors Cox and Goodman present tables which include composite data showing the marketing work performed in assembling materials for the example

---

[5]The flow charts and monographs for the 43 building products studied are presented in Cox and Goodman, *Channels and Flows in the Marketing of House-Building Materials*, Vol. II.

A PORTION OF FLOW CHART FOR WINDOW UNITS (EXAMPLE)

TIME	FORM	PLACE (1)	FACILITY	ACTIVITY	FACILITY	ACTIVITY	DIST.	PRODUCT	LOCATION FACILITY	MOVEMENT FACILITY	PRODUCT	MOVEMENT FACILITY	VALUE	FEES
			LOCATION		MOVEMENT			OPERATIONAL CONTROL			OWNERSHIP			
0.	Window unit (56+)	Phila.	Site	Unloading	Truck	LMU	L	Builder	Builder	Retailer	Builder	Retailer	17.64	
1			Warehouse	Storage				Retailer	Retailer	Retailer	Retailer	Retailer		
2														
3														
4														
5														
6			Warehouse	Storage										
7	Window unit (56#)		Shop	Assembly										
8	Glazed Sash (21#)		Warehouse	Storage										
57			Warehouse	Storage										
58			Siding	Unloading	RR-CLS	U		Retailer	Retailer	Retailer	Retailer	Railroad	4.03 delvd.	
59		Phila.	Siding	Unloading		MU	1005	Railroad	Retailer	Railroad	Jobber	Railroad		
60		In transit				M								
69		In transit												
70	Glazed Sash (21#)	Riverton Ia.	Siding	Loading	RR-CLS	L		Railroad	Millwk. mfr.	Railroad	Jobber	Railroad	3.84 frt. allow'd; 3.70 mill net	
71			Factory	Glazing				Millwk. mfr.	Millwk. mfr.	Millwk. mfr.	Millwk. mfr.			
72	Open sash, 6 ft. b.m. net (10#)			Storage										
73	Open sash			Mfg. sash									2.19	
74	Sash in process													
86	Sash in process			Mfg. sash										
87	Cut stock			Storage										
115			Warehouse	Storage										
116	Cut stock		Factory	Cutting										
117	8½ ft. b.m. #2 shop, KD p.p. 6/4 S2S to 1 3/32, lg.7#		Warehouse	Storage										
176			Warehouse	Storage										
177		Riverton Ia.	Siding	Unloading	RR-CLS	MU	2277	Millwk. mfr.	Millwk. mfr.	Millwk. mfr.	Millwk. mfr.	Railroad	1.166	
178		In transit			Railroad	M		Railroad	Railroad	Railroad		Railroad		
179														
180														.208 @$1.08 cwt. plus tax
181														

(1) All names of places other than Philadelphia are fictitious to avoid disclosure.

Figure 9 — A PORTION OF FLOW CHART FOR WINDOW UNITS

Source: Reavis Cox and Charles S. Goodman, "Marketing of Housebuilding Materials," *Journal of Marketing*, national quarterly publication of the American Marketing Association, Vol. XXI (July, 1956), p. 42.

house.[6] These tables were constructed by taking relevant data from the flow charts on analyzed products and analyzed antecedents. The data were then supplemented by estimates of the marketing work performed for (a) unanalyzed antecedents of the analyzed products and (b) the materials and products that were not analyzed.

Methodology. The bulk of the data used by Professors Cox and Goodman were obtained from original sources, i.e., from buyers, sellers, processors, and handlers of the building materials studied. Starting with builders active in the Philadelphia area, members of the staff organized by Professors Cox and Goodman collected the desired information by working backward through marketing agencies and processors to the extractors of the basic raw materials.

On the whole, Professors Cox and Goodman write, individuals connected with the building-materials industry were willing to exert much effort in order to supply the information called for by the framework of the flow chart and the product monograph. They point out, however, that in some instances the persons interviewed did not have available to them appropriate records and could report only their impressions rather than precise facts.

Analysis Permitted by the Cox and Goodman Approach. Using the mass of information included in the flow charts and the product monographs, Professors Cox and Goodman were able to conclude their study with a number of judgments as to (1) the efficiency of the marketing work performed in assembling the building materials for the example house and (2) the desirability of adopting certain proposals for reducing the cost of housing.

The final phase of the study presented overall comments, from the point of view of marketing efficiency, on:

1. The organization of the housebuilding materials industry.
2. The rationale of the transportation of building materials, e.g., use of nearby sources of supply, extent of crosshauling and backhauling.
3. The extent to which materials are handled in optimum quantities.
4. The extent to which storage costs are reduced.
5. The flexibility of marketing methods used by the building materials industry, e.g., responsiveness to small cost differences and development of drop shipping.

---

[6]See Reavis Cox and Charles S. Goodman, "Marketing of Housebuilding Materials,"*Journal of Marketing*, national quarterly publication of the American Marketing Association, Vol. XXI (July, 1956), pp. 45 and 46.

In addition to these comments, Professors Cox and Goodman used their data to present judgments on whether more integration in the building material industry, modular dimensions,[7] and prefabrication were likely to reduce the cost of houses.

Breyer Study: Quantitative Systemic Analysis and Control

Like Professors Cox and Goodman, Professor Breyer has interested himself in the performance of channels of marketing, particularly the control of the operations of these channels. His study, *Quantitative Systemic Analysis and Control*, aims to develop concepts and quantitative methods of analysis designed to facilitate control of the operations of marketing channels with a view to increasing their efficiency.

The Systemic Approach. Although Professor Breyer's study focuses on the control of marketing channels, he emphasizes that the study represents an example of the systemic approach to marketing. Breyer writes that this approach is "an approach to the study of marketing that is focused primarily on an integral part of the marketing institution (a 'system') that is of channel dimension and takes care of a full 'cycle' of marketing."[8]

In Breyer's opinion a channel or group of channels constitute marketing systems because an interdependence exists among the business units which comprise them. This interdependence arises out of the fact that the *raison d'etre* of the business units comprising a channel is to take care of "the full marketing channel," i.e., perform the marketing work necessary to move goods from producer to consumer.[9]

In Breyer's judgment the systemic approach is suitable for the study of all aspects of marketing. He states that the more important channel systems deserve individual study as "distinct operating units" of the entire marketing organization of an economy. Breyer goes on to write:

> The peculiar theoretical framework of each such major system needs to be developed; our body of marketing "principles" needs to

---

[7]Modular dimensions are a method of standardization which seems to offer advantages in manufacturing and in the actual construction of a house. Theoretically modular dimensions are supposed to help to set up longer production runs in the factories and reduce both the waste of materials on the site and some amount of cutting and fitting.

[8]Ralph F. Breyer, *Quantitative Systemic Analysis and Control: Study No. 1 — Channel and Channel Group Costing* (Philadelphia: published by the author, 1949), p. 8.

[9]The combined business units of marketing channels, Breyer writes, represent *unique systems* in that each possesses some peculiar pattern of sizes and concerns, or product assemblies, or of geographical dispersion, or of common interests among the concerns, or distinctive combinations of such patterns.

be reoriented to this pattern of systems, with a more realistic treatment of the channel structure of marketing; our research into price-making processes must not only strive to explain pricing and prices in terms of channels *in general* but it must strive to formulate the distinctive processes, and it is almost bound to be in some significant degree distinctive, for *each* of such major systems. This is not to argue that the *general* theory, the *general* principle, the *general* management methods, and so on, are not valid within prescribed and recognized limits and should be discarded, but rather that they need refinement that shapes them neatly to the actual situations in marketing. And the unalterable fact is that the marketing institution is made up of a variegated pattern of such systems, that they do the work of marketing, and that therefore both marketing scholars as well as practitioners must deal with these many different systems and not merely with a sort of amalgam of them whose analysis gives us findings that fit none of them truly. If the present study will serve in some way to make the students of marketing properly aware of this need for the "systemic approach" to the practical and theoretical study of marketing, it will have fully served its purpose. . . .[10]

The Nature of Systemic Control. In order to permit analysis and control of the operations of a channel system, Breyer's study aims to develop appropriate quantitative methods. These seek to measure the overall performance of marketing systems and to permit quantitative subanalyses of such systems which will uncover and measure points of weakness and strength.

When Breyer discusses channel control, he has in mind a specific type of marketing channel whose operations are to be analyzed and controlled. He has named this channel the unit marketing channel. This channel is composed of business units, engaged in marketing, having a distinct business identity or name or a distinct business location, regardless of common ownership. Thus, Breyer writes, a wholesale concern known as "A" and a retail concern known as "B," although owned by the same individual, are each given separate recognition as an integral part of the unit marketing channel even though they might occupy the same quarters. In Breyer's terminology a combination of two or more unit marketing channels constitute a unit marketing channel group.[11]

---

[10]Breyer, *Quantitative Systemic Analysis and Control: Study No. 1 — Channel and Channel Group Costing*, pp. 8–9.

[11]Breyer uses the unit marketing channel rather than the "traditional" concept of the channel — an ordered series of types of trading concerns which move goods from producers to consumers — because, he writes, it has shortcomings for purposes of channel analysis and control. Among the shortcomings he cites are: (1) the types of

Since most unit marketing channels consist of multiple ownerships, Breyer states, effective systemic analysis and control requires that the business units comprising these systems establish an authority with at least limited powers to manage the channel or channel group. As Breyer conceives it, such a managerial body would, "ideally," perform the following functions:

1. Establish the basic objectives for the channel system.
2. Determine the activities required to accomplish these goals.
3. Allocate these activities among the enterprises composing the system, i.e., determine which enterprises would perform specific activities such as, for example, packaging.
4. Establish a system for controlling the channel's operations.

Effective systemic control, Breyer believes, requires that the objectives established for the channel or channel group be paramount, with the objectives of the individual business units, whether independently owned or not, being derived from them. Actual control of the system's operations designed to achieve the overall objectives, he points out, requires that quantitative standards be established for the system as a whole. Actual performance of the system would then be compared against these standards and remedial action taken where warranted. Operating standards, Breyer emphasizes, should not be a mere sum of the standards of the individual enterprises composing the channel or channel group. For effective systemic control the standards for the individual establishments should be determined, at least in part, by overall channel considerations.

Breyer is very much aware of the difficulty of achieving effective systemic control. Among the difficulties he cites are:

---

business units employed are too crude for channel analysis and control, (2) the establishment of types of business units involves considerable arbitrary classification of trading enterprises, and (3) certain significant phases of channel control sometimes involve nontrading enterprises. These business units, however, Breyers states, are excluded from the traditional concept of the channel.

The unit marketing channel is composed of several constituent channels. The unit goods channel is a constituent channel that is formed by the "route" followed by the physical movement of the goods. The unit sales channel is formed by the "route" followed by the trading contacts. The unit selling channel is formed by the "flow" of the selling and/or buying effort. The unit transfer channel is formed by the "route" taken by the actual transfers of title to goods.

Breyer regards the enterprise marketing channel, a channel conceived in terms of specific, independently-owned business entities, as his primary channel concept. He holds this view because, he states, the enterprises composing the enterprise marketing channel are the initiating, financing, and risking agencies of marketing. The enterprise marketing channel, however, is not appropriate for quantitative systemic analysis and control, Breyer asserts, because such analysis and control needs to focus on individual business units regardless of common ownership.

1. Effective control of nonintegrated channels is likely to lead to larger profits for the aggregate system; however, since not all business units in the system are likely to benefit, the owners of such enterprises, Breyer believes, would probably be unwilling to cooperate with the system's managerial and control authority.
2. Even if the component business units cooperate, the nature of the situation is such that it is difficult to coordinate the successive activities of different and physically separate enterprises.

In Breyer's opinion a number of conditions facilitate the establishment of an effective channel control mechanism. Those that he cites are:

1. A high degree of integration in a channel or channel group.
2. A long record of cooperation among the independent owners in a channel.
3. Channels that are likely to persist for a long time and which are characterized by stable trading characteristics.
4. A situation in which most of the business units in a channel handle a limited number and similar group of products.
5. A reasonably large dollar volume handled in the channel by each of its business units and accounting for a significant percentage of each.
6. A minimum of independent nontrading business units which, because they usually have little at stake in any one channel, are not likely to cooperate effectively with any systemic arrangement.
7. A short and simple channel which, by making the task of analysis and control easier, increases the opportunity for such a program.

Principal Kinds of Systemic Cost Analysis. Breyer's study has led him to the conclusion that, with a few exceptions, the types of cost analysis which are significant for systemic control are the same as those which have been employed by individual business enterprises. Among these are product, customer, functional, and order-size cost analyses.

The one type of systemic cost analysis that has no counterpart in cost analysis for the single enterprise is what Breyer terms "nexus" cost analysis. This type of analysis determines the aggregate cost of complementary marketing activities of two business units of a specific channel, e.g., the selling work of a wholesaler directed at a retailer and the buying work of this retailer performed in making his purchases from the above mentioned wholesaler.

In order to compute costs for the various kinds of systemic cost analyses, the analyst first determines the relevant costs for the individual enterprises comprising the system being studied. Breyer states that the costing methods for this purpose are the familiar distribution cost analysis techniques used by individual marketing concerns. When this information has been obtained, the individual enterprise cost data are then added to establish the channel or channel group cost figures that are desired.

Breyer's first illustration shows how a cost analysis is made for a single, simple channel selling only one product to one ultimate consumer. In this example he shows how total channel costs for a single function, computation of costs for a channel segment, for various order sizes, and the like are carried out. He then demonstrates the costing methods that can be used when analyzing more complex channels having agents and nontrading institutions in them. Finally, Breyer discusses the techniques to be used in cost analysis for channels.[12]

The cost data for enterprises used in systemic analysis exclude the profits of the individual marketing firm. That is, systemic costs represent an accumulation of the operating costs of the enterprises which comprise a given system. Breyer views an entire marketing channel or channel group as an apparatus whose costs are those incurred by the owners of the various parts of the mechanism and not by the consuming public. Hence, Breyer writes, systemic costs serve to show the executives of the various business units their combined operating costs for moving goods from producer to consumer by means of the channel or channel group.

While Breyer is convinced of the utility to marketing of quantitative systemic analysis and control, the final comments of his study indicate that he is pessimistic as to the likelihood that this type of analysis and control will be widely accepted in the near future. His view stems essentially from two conclusions:

1. Channel and channel group costing apparently have little promise for the numerous channels which include small retail business enterprises.
2. The fact that most channels consist of multiple ownerships weakens the incentive to undertake quantitative systemic analysis and control since the benefits that each enterprise can gain are uncertain, depending largely upon its strategy and maneuvering within the framework of overall cooperation.

---

[12]See Breyer, *Quantitative Systemic Analysis and Control: Study No. 1 — Channel and Channel Group Costing*, Chapters 5–7.

Evaluation

The study conducted by Professors Cox and Goodman had as its ultimate objective the reduction in the cost of homes. It aimed to contribute to this result by suggesting ways in which the marketing of housebuilding materials could be made more efficient and, thus, diminish this component of the total cost of a house.

As indicated earlier in this chapter, financial limitations restricted the study to one type of house constructed on a site in Philadelphia. The authors believe that their study reveals much about the efficiency of the marketing of housebuilding materials entering this area. As such the study is, of course, of value to individuals involved in these marketing activities as well as builders constructing homes in Philadelphia.

The study is also useful because it can be said to be a successful experiment in research methodology. That is, the procedures and tools of analysis developed by Professors Cox and Goodman are likely to prove useful to analysts in conducting similar studies for the building materials industry and for other industries as well.

As demonstrated by Professors Cox and Goodman, their measures of marketing work do, in fact, indicate the real burdens imposed by several marketing flows associated with the movement of building materials through distribution channels. The flow charts together with the product monographs provide substantial information which is necessary for evaluating the efficiency of marketing work performed in marketing channels.

Examination of the Cox and Goodman conclusions as to the effectiveness of the flows for building materials reveals that their procedures and analytical tools provided them with sufficient data to make informative comments about many facets of the efficiency question they studied. The following illustrate the range of conclusions that Cox and Goodman were able to make using the procedures and tools of analysis developed for their Philadelphia study:

1. There is no evidence to support a charge that had been made to the effect that there was much unnecessary transportation of building materials.
2. Crosshauling and backhauling of building materials are rare.
3. A substantial proportion of the ton-miles performed for building materials is done in truckloads, carloads, and bargeloads rather than in part loads.
4. The bulk of the storage of building materials occurs when storage is cheapest. It may be possible to reduce the amount of storage of finished goods within the Philadelphia area.

5. The building-materials industries have gone far in the direction of applying the desirable principle of massed reserves to their storage problem.[13]

6. Individuals involved in the marketing and use of housebuilding materials are flexible in the methods they use and will shift in response to moderate price and cost advantages. For example, drop shipping is frequently used when this practice is feasible.

7. There is much evidence to support the belief that substantially excessive costs in the various flows cannot long continue. Cox and Goodman have concluded that any individual in any flow who wants to absorb a task usually performed by others can ordinarily work out a transaction of the kind he wants with appropriate adjustments in price.

8. Integration, modular dimensions, and prefabrication are proposals that have been made for reducing the cost of homes. The detailed type of analysis performed by Professors Cox and Goodman enabled them to come to conclusions about the first two of these proposals and to speculate about the third. On the basis of their study they doubted that integration, i.e., a reduction in the number of business entities, could be extended in the channels carrying housebuilding materials into Philadelphia. They based this conclusion on the knowledge that:
   a. The number of raw materials used was large.
   b. The points of origin of these raw materials were many and dispersed.
   c. There are substantial differences in the processes of handling and fabricating the raw materials.

9. Use of modular dimensions, Cox and Goodman concluded, could contribute to a reduction in the cost of houses; but, they comment, the beneficial effect of this innovation would likely be felt only in the long run.

It is clear from the above that the techniques and analytical tools developed by Professors Cox and Goodman were adequate to enable them to come to useful conclusions about a broad range of questions comprising the efficiency problem they studied. However, their study did not enable them to reach conclusions on a few aspects of the problem.

On the basis of their data Cox and Goodman could only speculate as to the effect of prefabrication on marketing costs. After weighing the pertinent data, they hypothesized that prefabrication might add to the marketing work and cost associated with the flows of house-

---

[13]Under the principle of massed reserves, goods are held for a group of distributors and users by a few agencies. This principle results in a reduction in the cost of storage because total stocks can be smaller when they are centralized than when they are dispersed.

building materials rather than reduce them. With respect to transportation, Cox and Goodman were unable to determine whether the industry manifested inefficiency in that (1) it transported products that included substantial amounts of waste materials and (2) it failed to minimize the number of movements of materials.[14]

While Cox and Goodman doubted that the industry had applied the principle of postponement[15] as fully as it might, they were unable to come to a definite conclusion on this question. This question, they state, required even more detailed analysis than they were able to perform.

Professor Breyer's contribution centers on the systemic approach and the development of costing techniques and concepts for the analysis and control of channel operations. In proposing that it is desirable to develop marketing theories and principles from the point of view of channel systems, Breyer may be said to be extending the institutional approach so that it encompasses the study of combinations of marketing institutions. In view of the fact that the efficiency as well as the success of marketing depends on the coordinated activities of channel agencies, it makes sense to conceive of these channels as systems and to regard them as a useful point of view from which to study marketing.

As indicated earlier in this chapter, Breyer's study focuses on only one aspect of the systemic approach, i.e., the analysis and control of channel systems. In this area he has made a substantial contribution by pointing out the advantage to be derived from systemic analysis and control and demonstrating the costing techniques for such analysis and control.

The usefulness of Breyer's contribution to fully integrated channels and government marketing officials is unmistakable. Both interests are concerned with the efficiency of marketing operations beyond the individual enterprise.

Breyer's approach is also potentially useful to other marketing agencies. For example, a producer using several marketing channels might employ systemic analysis as a basis for deciding which types of channels to drop and which to retain. Moreover, enlightened inde-

---

[14]Reducing the number of movements of materials, of course, reduces the number of loadings and unloadings.

[15]The principle of postponement was developed by Reavis Cox and Wroe Alderson. This principle states that marketing efficiency is enhanced if business entities postpone changes in form and identity of products to the latest possible point in the marketing flow and postpone changes in inventory location to the latest possible point in time. This principle is designed to avoid or reduce the cost of mistaken commitments.

pendent agencies composing nonintegrated channels could use systemic analysis for shifting marketing functions among agencies so as to improve efficiency. For example, compilation of channel costs for such functions as packaging, credit, and promotion might reveal that it would be worthwhile to eliminate, consolidate, or transfer certain functions.

The contributions by Cox, Goodman, and Breyer are alike in that they are concerned with the efficiency of work performed by marketing channels. They differ in that the Cox and Goodman approach uses real magnitudes while Breyer uses money measurements as the basis for analysis and control. Both pioneering approaches, however, constitute substantially useful contributions in that they present concepts, procedures, and analytical techniques for analyzing and improving the efficiency of work performed by marketing channels.

Chapter 9

SUMMARY AND CONCLUSIONS

The theorists whose approaches have been examined in previous chapters have concentrated on different aspects of marketing or on methods of analysis intended to be useful to marketing students and practitioners. These theorists have studied the movement of retail trade, social physics, game theory, interregional and intraregional marketing, organized behavior systems and marketing behavior, marketing functions, and the efficiency of marketing channels.

In using their respective approaches these theorists have sought to attain a number of objectives. Reilly and Converse have aimed at unearthing numerical formulas which would enable retailers to predict the division of shopping goods trade among competing cities or towns. In essence the social physicists have similar objectives in that they wish to develop numerical formulas which have predictive utility, but they are also interested in broader aspects of human behavior.

The game theorists seek to build an analytical method which would specify rational conduct in conflict situations and which would permit prediction of the gains or losses incurred by players, e.g., businessmen, in such situations. Grether has focused on interregional and intraregional marketing in his effort to develop applied marketing theories which (1) provide a conceptual framework within which the facts of marketing can be organized and (2) present a realistic explanation of particular aspects of marketing.

McGarry's theoretical objective has been to develop carefully reasoned and refined statements which will accurately describe marketing situations and assist in explaining what is happening in marketing. In pursuance of this objective he has concentrated on attempting to understand the role of marketing in any economy and the functions which marketing must perform. Alderson has concerned himself with the overall marketing system and has sought to provide students and practitioners with perspective about the operation of this system and its components.

The approaches of Cox, Goodman, and Breyer concentrate on improving the efficiency of marketing channels. Toward this end they have sought to develop useful concepts and analytical techniques.

The different approaches used by these students can be summarized as follows:

Reilly, Converse, Stewart, and Warntz have utilized regression analysis in order to uncover the numerical formulas they seek. The game theorists use logic and mathematics in pursuance of their normative and predictive objectives.

The logic and tools of economic analysis play the major role in the development of Grether's theory of interregional marketing. As for his intraregional marketing theory, his method might be termed qualitative multiple-correlation analysis since it focuses on the factors which determine the size of market areas.

As used by McGarry, the functional approach appears to be largely speculative and is based at least in part on limited deduction. That is, speculative generalizations are made, based on facts which are only known to be applicable to specific situations, and deductions are then made from these speculations or from "facts" which appear to be self-evident.

The methodology of Alderson's functionalist approach is difficult to specify because practically no documentation appears in his *Marketing Behavior and Executive Action*. The insights and hypotheses presented in this volume, however, appear to emanate from his rich experience and from a wide reading of relevant literature.

Having concluded that for many purposes it is useful to evaluate the efficiency of marketing channels in real terms, Cox and Goodman develop concepts and tools of analysis which permit the measurement and analysis of the real work performed by marketing channels. For his part, Breyer emphasizes the usefulness of studying many aspects of marketing from the point of view of channels of distribution, i.e., the systemic approach. Breyer's particular interest is the development of concepts and analytical techniques designed to permit the use of distribution cost analysis with respect to the work of groups of channels and segments thereof.

The theorists included in this study have attained their objectives in varying degrees. With respect to the "laws" of retail gravitation, no evidence has been presented which would lead to a rejection of Reilly's basic formula, $B_a/B_b = (P_a/P_b) (D_b/D_a)^2$. However, this formula and the others developed by Converse have not been tested on representative samples over time and, therefore, cannot yet be accepted as marketing laws.

While the objectives of social physics are of interest to marketing study, the development of this discipline has not yet progressed to the point where it has made a tangible contribution to marketing study and practice; and game theory has yet to be developed to the point where it can cope with the complicated conflict marketing situations which occur in the work-a-day world.

In formulating his theory of interregional marketing Grether has modified the purely competitive theory of international trade by such observed factors as successfully differentiated products and public and private barriers to interregional marketing. However, this theory is largely a logical explanation developed from assumptions, and it is not known to what extent the resultant explanation fits the facts of interregional marketing.

Grether's theory of interregional marketing is illuminating because it states in general terms the effect of the numerous factors involved in the determination of market areas. Moreover, it contributes to understanding by revealing the differences in the kinds of factors which are important in the determination of the market areas of various types of sellers. In its present form Grether's qualitative theory of market area determination represents a useful beginning toward the ultimate development of a more informative theory.

There appears to be considerable plausibility to much of McGarry's functional concepts and analysis. In general, however, the extent to which his largely speculative and deductive contribution portrays and understands marketing reality is not known.

Alderson's approach certainly provides perspective with respect to the structure and functioning of organized behavior systems and the overall marketing system. However, it is uncertain how accurate this perspective is. This is so because, as Alderson points out, much of his contribution consists of hypotheses which need to be tested.

Cox and Goodman have contributed useful concepts and study procedures aimed at (1) measuring the real work performed by marketing channels and (2) facilitating an evaluation of the efficiency of this work. Their pioneering investigation of the marketing of housebuilding materials constitutes a useful model of the kind of study that can be made in evaluating the efficiency of marketing channels in other industries.

Breyer's emphasis on the systemic approach is, of course, useful for the study, practice, and social analysis of marketing. With respect to the analysis and control of channel systems, he has made a contribution by pointing out the advantages of quantitative systemic analysis and control and by demonstrating the costing techniques for such analysis and control.

The evaluation of these various theoretical approaches leads to the conclusion that none has produced acceptable, empirically valid marketing theory. This, then, answers the first question posed by this study: What progress has been achieved in the development of marketing theory through use of certain major theoretical approaches?

The second question posed by this study was: How can marketing theory best be developed in the future? With respect to this question it should first be noted that the fact that none of the approaches evaluated above has yielded empirically valid marketing theory does not necessarily mean that they are incapable of doing so. Rather, this situation may reflect the fact that an approach has not been in use long enough or that the theorist using it did not have the resources required to conduct the research necessary for the proper use of his approach.[1]

Of the various approaches examined in this study, those of Reilly and Converse and of the social physicists appear to be the most promising for the future development of marketing theory. Both approaches utilize the empirical method of inquiry and are most likely to yield quantitative theories of the type which the writer believes should be included in a science of marketing.

The deductive approach of economic theory used by Grether appears to exaggerate the logical and economic bases of human behavior. This approach, however, may be useful in suggesting rules of action for inclusion in a science of marketing.

As for mathematical models of the game theory type, the problem is one of constructing models which can deal with the complexities of the real world. A major handicap associated with such models is that they are either based on only a few of the relevant empirical assumptions or some of the assumptions do not correspond with the existing empirical facts.

The writer's objection to the functional approach, as it is used by McGarry, is that it relies too heavily on deduction and speculation.

---

[1] It will be recalled that the study presupposes that the development of marketing theory is possible.

Somewhat similar comments can be made with respect to the product of Alderson's approach at this stage of its development.

Breyer's systemic approach has not yet been employed beyond his application of the approach to the analysis of distribution costs on a channel-wide basis. However, this approach presently appears to be more of a point of view rather than a method for developing marketing theory. The analytical method used by Cox and Goodman, though not a technique for developing marketing theory, has been demonstrated to be a useful model for analyzing the efficiency of work performed by marketing channels.

The writer's predilection for the empirical approach used by Reilly, Converse, and the social physicists stems from his concept of marketing theory. Theory, in the writer's view, has a useful purpose in aiding student understanding of what is actually going on in marketing and in enabling practitioners and government officials to make predictions about and to control marketing phenomena.

Therefore, a marketing theory should be such that it explains the variation of some marketing phenomena, e.g., sales of a product and size of market areas. Ideally a marketing theory should take the form of an equation relating a dependent variable to one or more independent variables. Moreover, a causal relationship needs to be demonstrated between the dependent and independent variables.

A marketing theory should be such as to yield accurate probability predictions about variation in the dependent variable on which it focuses. An explanatory statement or equation which does not meet this specification is here regarded not as theory but as speculation.

Reilly's formula, for example, would be more acceptable as a marketing theory if it enabled one to make accurate predictions, perhaps 7 times out of 10, of the range within which shopping-goods trade was divided between two trading centers.

An acceptable marketing theory would be additionally useful for purposes of control. This is so because the demonstrated causal relationship between dependent and independent variables might enable a marketing executive to bring about desired changes in the dependent variable by manipulating one or more of the independent variables, e.g., increasing sales (the dependent variable) by changing the marketing mix (the independent variables). A marketing theory would become a law if it were improved to the point where its predictions were perfectly accurate over time.

At this juncture there appears to be no way of avoiding the laborious empirical method in discovering marketing theory. The complexities of marketing phenomena appear, thus far, to have defied the logic of the deductive approach and the selected assumptions of mathematical models.

If, for example, marketing students wish to generalize about consumer buying behavior, it does not contribute to our knowledge of marketing to argue speculatively that the consumer is more rational than emotional, or vice versa. Rather, it is necessary that adequate funds be secured and a technique be developed for obtaining this information from a representative sample of consumers; and we are likely to discover that the central tendency of consumer behavior is some combination of rationality, emotion, and impulse and that the central tendency differs for different products, e.g., expensive appliances as compared with relatively inexpensive articles.

Of the various theoretical approaches evaluated in this study, only Reilly and the social physicists have restricted themselves to the discovery of theory through resort to empirical fact. In the writer's opinion the search for quantitative marketing theories should utilize these approaches. That is, the data of marketing and related fields should be studied for the discovery of regression equations and empirical regularities.

In using these approaches the rules of scholarly evidence should be kept in mind. Generalizations (central tendencies), theories, or laws are acceptable only after they have been found to be valid with respect to representative samples over time. Lacking such substantiation, they need to be regarded and presented as ephemeral findings or speculations. The writer speculates that many of the invalid deductions, the inaccurate speculations, and the generalizations made from inadequate evidence, which are found in marketing literature, stem not so much from ignorance of the rules of scholarly evidence but, rather, are the result of the lack of the resources needed to obtain the desired information.

In addition to believing that marketing science should be based on empirical fact, the writer believes that marketing should be viewed as a social science. In so viewing marketing it is believed that students working toward the development of marketing theory should utilize useful data from other social science areas, such as sociology, psychology, economics, anthropology, and political science.

BIBLIOGRAPHY

Books

Alderson, Wroe. "Areas for Basic Research in Marketing." Philadelphia, 1957. (Mimeographed pamphlet.)

—————. *Marketing Behavior and Executive Action.* Homewood, Illinois: Richard D. Irwin, Inc., 1957.

—————. "Problem Solving and Marketing Science." Philadelphia: Charles Coolidge Parlin Memorial Lecture, 1954.

Argyris, Chris, *et. al. Social Science Approaches to Business Behavior.* Homewood, Illinois: Richard D. Irwin, Inc., 1961.

Bakken, Henry H. *Theory of Markets and Marketing.* Madison: Mimir Publishers, Inc., 1953.

Baldwin, James M. (ed.). *Dictionary of Philosophy and Psychology.* Vol. I. New York: Peter Smith, 1940.

Bartels, Robert. *The Development of Marketing Thought.* Homewood, Illinois: Richard D. Irwin, Inc., 1962.

—————. "The Dimensions of Marketing Thought." E. J. Kelley and W. Lazer (eds.). *Managerial Marketing: Perspectives and Viewpoints.* Homewood, Illinois: Richard D. Irwin, Inc., 1958.

—————. "Marketing Literature — Development and Appraisal." Unpublished Ph.D. dissertation, Ohio State University, 1941.

Bass, Frank M., *et. al. Mathematical Models and Methods in Marketing.* Homewood, Illinois: Richard D. Irwin, Inc., 1961.

Beach, Earl F. *Economic Models.* New York: John Wiley & Sons, Inc., 1957.

A Bibliography of Theory and Research Techniques in the Field of Human Motivation. New York: Advertising Research Foundation, 1956.

Blackwell, D. H., and M. A. Girschick. *Theory of Games and Statistical Decisions.* New York: John Wiley & Sons, Inc., 1954.

137

Braithwaite, R. B. *Scientific Explanation*. Cambridge: Cambridge University Press, 1953.

Breyer, Ralph F. *Marketing Institution*. New York: McGraw-Hill Book Company, Inc., 1934.

——————. "Quantitative Systemic Analysis and Control: Study No. 1 — Channel and Channel Group Costing." Philadelphia: Published by the author, 1949. (Photo-offset.)

Bushaw, D. W. *Introduction to Mathematical Economics*. Homewood, Illinois: Richard D. Irwin, Inc., 1957.

Bye, Raymond T. *Principles of Economics*, Fifth Edition. New York: Appleton-Century-Crofts, Inc., 1956.

Cherington, Paul T. *The Elements of Marketing*. New York: The Macmillan Co., 1920.

Churchman, C. W., and R. L. Ackoff. *Methods of Inquiry*. St. Louis: Educational Publishers, 1950.

Clark, Lincoln H. (ed.). *Consumer Behavior*. 2 vols. New York: New York University Press, 1954.

Commons, John R. *Institutional Economics*. New York: The MacMillan Co., 1934.

Conant, James B. *Science and Common Sense*. New Haven: Yale University Press, 1951.

Converse, Paul D. *Retail Trade Areas in Illinois*. Business Study No. 6. Urbana: University of Illinois Press, 1946.

——————. *A Study of Retail Trade Areas in East Central Illinois*. Urbana: University of Illinois Press, 1943.

Converse, P. D., H. W. Huegy, and R. V. Mitchell. *The Elements of Marketing*, Sixth Edition. New York: Prentice Hall, Inc., 1958.

Cox, Reavis, and Wroe Alderson (eds.). *Theory in Marketing*. Homewood, Illinois: Richard D. Irwin, Inc., 1950.

Cox, Reavis, and Charles S. Goodman. "Channels and Flows in the Marketing of Housebuilding Materials." Philadelphia: Published by the authors, 1954. (Mimeographed.)

Dorfman, Robert, Paul A. Samuelson, and Robert M. Solow. *Linear Programming and Economic Analysis*. New York: McGraw-Hill Book Company, Inc., 1958.

Duddy, Edward A., and David A. Revzan. *Marketing: An Institutional Approach*. New York: McGraw-Hill Book Company, Inc., 1953.

Eiteman, W. J. *Price Determination: Business Practice versus Economic Theory*. Report No. 16. Ann Arbor: University of Michigan Bureau of Business Research, 1949.

Festinger, L. and D. Katz (eds.). *Research Methods in the Behavioral Sciences*. New York: Dryden Press, 1953.

Frank, R. E., A. A. Kuehn, and W. F. Massey. *Quantitative Techniques in Marketing Analysis*. Homewood, Illinois: Richard D. Irwin, Inc., 1962.

Goods, W. J., and P. K. Hatt. *Methods in Social Research*. New York: McGraw-Hill Book Company, Inc., 1952.

Hempel, Carl G. *Fundamentals of Concept Formation in Empirical Science*. Chicago: University of Chicago Press, 1952.

Hoover, Edgar M. *The Location of Economic Activity*. New York: McGraw-Hill Book Company, Inc., 1948.

Isard, Walter. *Location and Space Economy*. New York: John Wiley & Sons, Inc.; co-publisher, The Technological Press of M. I. T., 1956.

Klein, Lawrence R. *A Textbook of Econometrics*. Evanston, Illinois: Row, Peterson & Company, 1953.

Knauth, Oswald. *Business Practices, Trade Position, and Competition*. New York: Columbia University Press, 1956.

Lazer, William, and E. J. Kelley. *Interdisciplinary Contributions to Marketing Management*. East Lansing, Michigan: Michigan State University Press, 1959.

Lazersfeld, Paul F. (ed.). *Mathematical Thinking in the Social Sciences*. Glenco, Illinois: The Free Press of Glenco, Illinois, 1954.

Lever, E. A. *Advertising and Economic Theory*. New York: Oxford University Press, 1947.

Lippitt, Vernon G. *Determinants of Consumer Demand for House Furnishings and Equipment.* Cambridge: Harvard University Press, 1959.

Luce, Robert D., and Howard Raiffa. *Games and Decisions.* New York: John Wiley & Sons, Inc., 1957.

McInnes, William C. "A General Theory of Marketing." Unpublished Ph.D. dissertation, New York University, 1954.

McKinsey, J. C. C. *Introduction to the Theory of Games.* New York: McGraw-Hill Book Company, Inc., 1952.

Nagel, E. *Principles of the Theory of Probability.* Chicago: University of Chicago Press, 1939.

Neurath, O. *Foundations of the Social Sciences.* Chicago: University of Chicago Press, 1944.

Ohlin, Bertil. *Interregional and International Trade.* Cambridge: Harvard University Press, 1935.

Osterbind, Carter C. "An Appraisal of the Usefulness of Partial Equilibrium Theory in Marketing Research and Analysis." Unpublished Ph.D. dissertation, American University, 1953.

Otteson, Schuyler G. (ed.). *Marketing: Current Problems and Theories.* Bloomington: Indiana University Press, 1952.

Oxenfeldt, Alfred R. *Industrial Pricing and Market Practices.* New York: Prentice Hall, Inc., 1951.

Reilly, William J. *The Law of Retail Gravitation,* Second Edition. New York: Published by the author, 1953.

Rewolt, Stewart H. (ed.). *Frontiers in Marketing Thought.* Bloomington: Indiana University Press, 1954.

Riesman, David. *The Lonely Crowd.* In collaboration with Reuel Denny and Nathan Glazer. New Haven: Yale University Press, 1950.

Robbins, Lionel C. *An Essay on the Nature and Significance of Economic Science.* London: The MacMillan Co., 1940.

Rose, A. M. *Theory and Method in the Social Sciences.* Minneapolis: University of Minnesota Press, 1954.

Scott, Walter D. *The Theory and Practice of Advertising.* Boston: Small, Maynard & Co., 1908.

Shaw, Arch W. *Some Problems in Market Distribution*. Cambridge: Harvard University Press, 1915.

Shawver, Donald L. *The Development of Theories of Retail Price Determination in England and the United States*. Urbana: University of Illinois, 1956.

Shepherd, Geoffrey. *Marketing Farm Products — Economic Analysis*. Ames: Iowa State College Press, 1955.

Sherif, Muzafer, and Carolyn W. Sherif. *An Outline of Social Psychology*. New York: Harper & Brothers, 1956.

Sorokin, Pitirim A. *Fads and Foibles in Modern Sociology and Related Sciences*. Chicago: Henry Regnery Co., 1956.

Stonier, Alfred W., and Douglas C. Hague. *A Textbook of Economic Theory*, Third Edition. New York: Longmans, Green & Co., Inc., 1955.

Taylor, Weldon J. "A Critical Analysis of a Standard for Creating Scientific Objectives in the Study of Marketing and the Application of Such Standard to Contemporary Marketing Literature." Unpublished Ph.D. dissertation, New York University, 1955.

Thompson, Ralph B. *Marketing Theory: a selected and annotated bibliography*. Austin: University of Texas Press, 1958.

Tinter, Gerhard. *Mathematics and Statistics for Economists*. New York: Rinehart & Company, Inc., 1954.

Tosdal, Harry R. *Selling in Our Economy*. Homewood, Illinois: Richard D. Irwin, Inc., 1957.

Tull, Donald S. "An Examination of the Hypothesis that Advertising Has a Lagged Effect on Sales." Unpublished Ph.D. dissertation, University of Chicago, 1956.

Umemura, George M. "The Marketing Ideas of the Classical School." Unpublished Ph.D. dissertation, Indiana University, 1952.

Vaile, R. S., E. T. Grether, and R. Cox. *Marketing in the American Economy*. New York: The Ronald Press Company, 1952.

von Neumann, John, and Oskar Morgenstern. *Theory of Games and Economic Behavior*. Third Edition. Princeton: Princeton University Press, 1953.

Wales, Hugh G. (ed.). *Changing Perspectives in Marketing.* Urbana: University of Illinois Press, 1951.

Warner, W. Lloyd, M. Meeker, and K. Eells. *Social Class in America.* Chicago: Science Research Associates, 1949.

Weintraub, S. *Price Theory.* New York: Pitman Publishing Corp., 1949.

White, L. D. *The State of the Social Sciences.* Chicago: University of Chicago Press, 1956.

White, Percival. *Scientific Marketing Management.* New York: Harper & Brothers, 1927.

Wiener, Philip P. (ed.). *Readings in the Philosophy of Science.* New York: Charles Scribner's Sons, 1953.

Williams, J. D. *The Compleat Strategyst.* New York: McGraw-Hill Book Company, Inc., 1954.

Zaniecki, Florian. *Cultural Sciences.* Urbana: University of Illinois Press, 1952.

Zipf, George K. *Human Behavior and Least Effort.* Cambridge: Addison-Wesley Press, 1949.

Articles

Alderson, Wroe, and Reavis Cox. "Towards a Theory of Marketing," *Journal of Marketing* (October, 1948).

Alexis, Marcus. "Marketing Laws and Marketing Strategy," *Journal of Marketing* (October, 1962).

Allen, R. G. D. "Seasonal Variation in Retail Prices," *Economics* (February, 1954).

Anshen, Melvin. "Fundamental and Applied Research in Marketing," *Journal of Marketing* (January, 1955).

Applebaum, William, and Richard F. Spears. "Controlled Experimentation in Marketing Research," *Journal of Marketing* (April, 1951).

Balderston, F. E. "Assortment Choice in Wholesale and Retail Marketing," *Journal of Marketing* (October, 1950).

Barclay, William D. "A Probability Model for Early Prediction of New Product Market Success." *Journal of Marketing* (January, 1963).

Bartels, Robert. Review of Bakken's *Theory of Markets and Marketing, American Economic Review* (March, 1954).

Bartels, R. D. W. "Marketing Principles," *Journal of Marketing* (October, 1944).

——————. "Can Marketing Be a Science," *Journal of Marketing* (January, 1951).

——————. "Influences on the Development of Marketing Thought, 1900–1923," *Journal of Marketing* (July, 1951).

Baumol, W. J. "On the Role of Marketing Theory," *Journal of Marketing* (April, 1957).

Bilkey, Warren J. "The Vector Hypothesis of Consumer Behavior," *Journal of Marketing* (October, 1951).

——————. "A Psychological Approach to Consumer Behavior Analysis," *Journal of Marketing* (January, 1954).

Blankertz, Donald F. Review of Duddy and Revzan's "Marketing: An Institutional Approach," *Journal of Marketing* (October, 1953).

Bliss, Perry. "Non-Price Competition at the Department Store Level," *Journal of Marketing* (April, 1953).

Boulding, Kenneth S. "General Systems Theory — The Skeleton of Science," *Management Science* (April, 1956).

Brown, T. H. "Science, Statistics, and Business," *Harvard Business Review* (Autumn, 1937).

Brown, W. F. "The Determination of Factors Influencing Brand Choice," *Journal of Marketing* (April, 1950).

Bund, Henry, and James W. Carroll. "The Changing Role of the Marketing Function," *Journal of Marketing* (January, 1956).

Butler, B. F. "Progress in Deriving 'Marketing Laws' " *Journal of Marketing* (April 1961).

Buzzell, Robert D. "Is Marketing a Science," *Harvard Business Review* (January–February, 1963).

Buzzell, Robert D. and Charles C. Slater. "Decision Theory and Marketing Management," *Journal of Marketing* (July, 1962).

Carlson, Robert O. "How Can the Social Scientists Meet the Needs of Advertisers?" *Printers' Ink* (October 30, 1953).

Cassels, J. M. "The Significance of Early Economic Thought on Marketing," *Journal of Marketing* (October, 1936).

Chamberlin, Edward H. "The Product as an Economic Variable," *Quarterly Journal of Economics* (February, 1953).

Churchill, W. L. "Scientific Pricing," *American Marketing Journal* (January, 1935).

Conant, James B. "Science and the Practical Arts," *Harvard Business Review* (Autumn, 1947).

Converse Paul D. "New Laws of Retail Gravitation," *Journal of Marketing* (October, 1949).

——————. "The Development of the Science of Marketing — An Exploratory Survey," *Journal of Marketing* (July, 1945).

——————. "The Total Cost of Marketing," *Journal of Marketing* (April, 1946).

——————. "Who Does Basic Marketing Research?" *Journal of Marketing* (April, 1955).

——————. "Comment on Reynolds' Test of the Law of Retail Gravitation," *Journal of Marketing* (October, 1953).

——————. "The Retail Trade of a Satellite Town," *Opinion* (February, 1945).

Cowan, S. "An Example of Scientific Marketing Procedure," *Bulletin of the Taylor Society* (June, 1924).

Cox, Reavis. "Non-Price Competition and the Measurement of Prices," *Journal of Marketing* (April, 1946).

——————. "Dean Lockley's Advertising Principles," *Journal of Marketing* (April, 1955).

——————. "The Meaning and Measurement of Productivity in Distribution," *Journal of Marketing* (April, 1948).

Cox, Reavis, and Charles S. Goodman. "Marketing of House-Building Materials," *Journal of Marketing* (July, 1956).

Cross, Gordon B. "A Scientific Approach to Retail Pricing," *Journal of Retailing* (Fall, 1959).

Cross, James E. "Operations Research in Solving a Marketing Problem," *Journal of Marketing* (January, 1961).

Dow, Louis A. "Marketing Costs and Economic Theory," *Journal of Marketing* (April, 1955).

Due, John F. "A Theory of Retail Price Determination," *Southern Economic Journal* (January, 1941).

Edwards, Ward. "The Theory of Decision Making," *Psychological Bulletin* (July, 1954).

Farlow, A. C. "Creative Advertising in Scientific Marketing: Careless and Inefficient Advertising Results from Thinking of Markets as Places and Columns of Statistics Instead of as People and Individuals," *Western Advertising* (March, 1947).

Fishman, Leo. "Consumer Expectations and the Consumption Function," *Southern Economic Journal* (January, 1954).

Fisk, George. "A Conceptual Model for Studying Customer Images," *Journal of Retailing* (Winter, 1961–1962).

—————. "Toward a Theory of Leisure-Spending Behavior," *Journal of Marketing* (October, 1959).

Fourt, Louis A., and Joseph W. Woodlock. "Early Prediction of Market Success for New Grocery Products," *Journal of Marketing* (October, 1960).

Freeland, W. E. "Progress Towards Science in Marketing," *Bulletin of the Taylor Society* (October, 1926).

Freeland, Willard F. "Scientific Management in Marketing," *Journal of Marketing* (April, 1940).

Fulbrook, Earl S. "The Functional Concept in Marketing," *Journal of Marketing* (January, 1940).

Gardner, Burleigh B. "How the Social Sciences Are Used in Advertising," *Printers' Ink* (December 11, 1953).

Giles, R. "How Far Can We Apply the Scientific Method to Advertising?" *Advertising and Selling* (February 8, 1928).

Green, Paul E. "Bayesian Decision Theory in Pricing Strategy," *Journal of Marketing* (January, 1963).

Grogg, Charles I. "Diagnosis and the Developing Science of Business," *Harvard Business Review* (January, 1932).

Harper Marion, Jr. "A New Profession to Aid Marketing Management," *Journal of Marketing* (January, 1961).

Hawkins, Edward R. "Marketing and the Theory of Monopolistic Competition," *Journal of Marketing* (April, 1940).

——————. "Price Policies and Price Theory," *Journal of Marketing* (January, 1954).

Heiberg, Paul. "Has Engel's Law Its Limitations?" *Journal of the American Statistical Association* (June, 1931).

Herniter, Jerome D., and John F. Magee. "Customer Behavior as a Markov Process," *Operations Research* (January–February, 1961).

Hess, H. W. (ed.). "Scientific Distribution," *Annals of the American Academy of Political and Social Science* (September, 1924).

Holman, W. C. "Guess-Work in Advertising," *System* (August, 1913).

Hoving, Walter. "More Science in Merchandising," *Journal of Retailing* (July, 1926).

Hutchinson, K. D. "Marketing as a Science: An Appraisal," *Journal of Marketing* (January, 1952).

Jeuck, J. E. "Marketing Research — Milestone or Millstone," *Journal of Marketing* (April, 1953).

Jones, Fred M. "A New Interpretation of Marketing Functions," *Journal of Marketing* (January, 1943).

Jung, A. F. "Is Reilly's Law of Retail Gravitation Always True," *Journal of Marketing* (October, 1959).

Kelley, William T. "The Development of Early Thought in Marketing and Promotion," *Journal of Marketing* (July, 1956).

Kendall, Henry P. "Applying the Laws of Production to Distribution," *Printers' Ink* (May 15, 1950).

Knauth, Oswald. "Considerations in the Setting of Retail Prices," *Journal of Marketing* (July, 1949).

Lachman, Roy. "The Model in Theory Construction," *Psychological Review* (March, 1960).

Lavidge, Robert J., and Gary A. Steiner. "A Model for Predictive Measurements of Advertising Effectiveness," *Journal of Marketing* (October, 1961).

Lazer, William. "The Role of Models in Marketing," *Journal of Marketing* (April, 1962).

Lazer, William, and Eugene J. Kelley. "Interdisciplinary Horizons in Marketing," *Journal of Marketing* (October, 1960).

Lester, Richard. "Shortcomings of Marginal Analysis for Wage-Employment Problems," *American Economic Review* (March, 1946).

Lockley, Lawrence C. "Use of Principles in the Management of Advertising," *Journal of Marketing* (January, 1955).

Loeb, Benjamin. "The Use of Engel's Laws as a Basis for Predicting Consumer Expenditures," *Journal of Marketing* (July, 1955).

Lundberg, George. Review of Zipf's "Human Behavior and Least Effort," *Annals of the American Academy of Political and Social Science* (July, 1949).

Macneill, J. K. "Is Sales Management an Exact Science?" *Printers' Ink* (August 29, 1929).

Maffei, Richard B. "Can the Effect of Advertising on Brand Preferences be Predicted," *Journal of Retailing* (Spring, 1961).

Magee, John F. "Operations Research in Making Marketing Decisions," *Journal of Marketing* (October, 1960).

McGarry, Edmund D. "Elasticity of Demand as a Useful Marketing Concept," *American Economic Review*, Supplement (March, 1925).

——————. "The Contactual Function in Marketing," *Journal of Business* (April, 1951).

—————. "The Importance of Scientific Method in Advertising," *Journal of Marketing* (October, 1937).

—————. "Some Viewpoints in Marketing," *Journal of Marketing* (July, 1953).

—————. "The Propaganda Function in Marketing," *Journal of Marketing* (October, 1958).

—————. ⎮"Dean Lockley's Advertising Principles," *Journal of Marketing* (April, 1955).

McInnes, William. "The Analytic Problem Approach to Marketing," *Journal of Marketing* (October, 1956).

Miller, Neal E. "Social Science and the Art of Advertising," *Journal of Marketing* (January, 1950).

Newman, Joseph W. "New Insight, New Progress for Marketing," *Harvard Business Review* (November–December, 1957).

—————. "Put Research Into Marketing Decisions," *Harvard Business Review* (March–April, 1962).

Paranka, Stephen. "Marketing Predictions from Consumer Attitudinal Data," *Journal of Marketing* (July, 1960).

Politz, Alfred, and W. Edward Deming. "On the Necessity to Present Consumer Preferences as Predictions," *Journal of Marketing* (July, 1953).

Pyle, J. F. "Some Basic Concepts of Marketing," *Social Science* (July, 1939).

Raymond, Leonard J. "Direct Advertising Also Favors Scientific Marketing," *Journal of Marketing* (January, 1937).

Revzan, David A. Review of Cox and Alderson (eds.). "Theory in Marketing," *Journal of Marketing* (July, 1950).

Reynolds, Robert B. "A Test of the Law of Retail Gravitation," *Journal of Marketing* (January, 1953).

—————. "Rejoinder to Converse's Comment on Reynolds' Test of the Law of Retail Gravitation," *Journal of Marketing* (October, 1953).

Richards, Elizabeth A. "Operations Research or the Scientific Method," *Journal of Marketing* (October, 1954).

Roberts, Harry V. "Bayesian Statistics in Marketing," *Journal of Marketing* (January, 1963).

Ryan, F. W. "Functional Elements of Market Distribution," *Harvard Business Review* (January, 1935).

Schenk, Oliver B. "Mathematical Models for Market Simulation," *Journal of Marketing* (April, 1960).

Schwab, Victor. "The Ten Copy Appeals," *Printers' Ink* (December 17, 1943).

"Scientific Marketing — A New Branch of Education," *Outlook* (September 23, 1914).

Seelye, Alfred L. "The Importance of Economic Theory in Marketing Courses," *Journal of Marketing* (January, 1947).

Shaw, Arch W. "Some Problems in Market Distribution," *Quarterly Journal of Economics* (August, 1912).

Shepherd, Geoffrey. "Decentralization in Agricultural Marketing: Causes and Consequences," *Journal of Marketing* (April, 1942).

—————. "The Analytical Problem Approach to Marketing," *Journal of Marketing* (October, 1955).

Shubik, Martin. "The Uses of Game Theory in Management," *Management Science* (October, 1955).

Stainton, R. S. "Science in Marketing," *Journal of Marketing* (July, 1952).

Stewart, John Q. "Empirical Mathematical Rules Concerning the Distribution and Equilibrium of Population," *Geographical Review* (July, 1947).

—————. "A Basis for Social Physics," *Impact of Science on Society* (Summer, 1952).

—————. "Demographic Gravitation: Evidence and Applications," *Sociometry* (February–May, 1948).

Stewart, John Q., and William Warntz. "Macrogeography and Social Science," *Geographical Review* (April, 1958).

—————. "Physics of Population Distribution," *Journal of Regional Science* (Summer, 1958).

Strohkarck, Frank, and Katherine Phelps. "The Mechanics of Constructing a Market Area Map," *Journal of Marketing* (April, 1948).

Uhl, Kenneth P. "Factorial Design — Aid to Management," *Journal of Marketing* (January, 1962).

Vaile, Roland S. "Science Applied to Advertising," *Journal of Marketing* (July, 1955).

—————. "Towards a Theory of Marketing — A Comment," *Journal of Marketing* (April, 1949).

Vanderblue, Homer B. "The Functional Approach to the Study of Marketing," *Journal of Political Economy* (October, 1921).

Verdoorn, P. J. "Marketing from the Producer's Point of View," *Journal of Marketing* (January, 1956).

von Neumann, John. "Zur Theorie der Gesellschaftspiele," *Mathematische Annalen*, 100 (1928).

Walker, Amasa. "Scientific Management Applied to Commercial Enterprise," *Journal of Political Economy* (May, 1913).

Weber, John H. "Can Results of Sales Promotion Be Predicted?" *Journal of Marketing* (January, 1963).

Weinwurm, Ernest H. "Limitations of the Scientific Method in Management Science," *Management Science* (April, 1957).

Weiss, E. B. "Will Marketing Ever Become a Science?" *Advertising Age* (August 20, 1962).

Weld, L. D. H. "Marketing Functions and Mercantile Organizations," *American Economic Review* (June, 1917).

—————. Statement by the President of the American Marketing Society, *American Marketing Journal* (January, 1934).

Wineburgh, A. "Why Advertising Can't Be An Exact Science," *Printers' Ink* (March 14, 1935).

Winick, Charles. "Anthropology's Contributions to Marketing," *Journal of Marketing* (July, 1961).

INDEX

151